DIVINE IMPERATIVES

By

Herbert W. Byrne, Ed.D.

Copyright © 2004 by Herbert W. Byrne, Ed.D.

Divine Imperatives
by Herbert W. Byrne, Ed.D.

Printed in the United States of America

ISBN 1-594674-25-6

All rights reserved solely by the author. The author guarantees all contents are original and do not infringe upon the legal rights of any other person or work. No part of this book may be reproduced in any form without the permission of the author. The views expressed in this book are not necessarily those of the publisher.

Unless otherwise indicated, Bible quotations are taken from the King James Version. Copyright © 1964 By B. B. Kirkbride Bible Co., Inc.

www.xulonpress.com

Author of

A CHRISTIAN APPROACH TO EDUCATION
EDUCATION AND DIVINE REVELATION
IMPROVING CHURCH EDUCATION
ACHIEVING ACADEMIC INTEGRATION
CHALLENGING CONCEPTS FOR CHRISTIAN EDUCATION

Dedicated to my good friend,
Mike Sawyer

TABLE OF CONTENTS

Do You Believe in God?..9
Do You Know That You Will Face the Judgment? 11
Do You Know That We Are All Accountable to God?..................15
Have You Repented of Your Sins?..17
What Must I Do to Be Saved?..21
What Will You Do with Christ? 25
What Shall You Do to Inherit Eternal Life?..................................29
Have You Been Converted?..31
Have You Been Born Again? 35
Is Jesus Christ First in Your Life?..39
Are You Ready for the Second Coming of Christ? 41
How Shall We Escape If We Neglect So Great a Salvation? 45
Do You Know That You Need God's Holiness? 47
Are You Walking in the Way of Holiness?...................................49
Do You Know How to Live a Separated Life?.............................51
Do You Know How to Live a Clean Life? 55
What Does It Mean to be Perfect? 59
Do You Know That Sanctification Is The Will of God for All?....63

What Does It Mean to be Filled With the Holy Spirit?...................67
What Have You Given to God?..69
Do You Know God's Plan for Your Life? 73
Do You Know God's Plan of the Ages?..75

DO YOU BELIEVE IN GOD?
Gen 1:1: Psa 53:1

Do you believe that God exists? This is by far the most important question a person can ask? Its answer determines one's quality of life and destiny. It is a question for which an answer is required and forms one of God's greatest imperatives. The Bible declares, "The fool hath said in his heart, there is no God." (Psa 53:1)

Throughout the ages, the history of mankind reveals that most believe in a Supreme Being, although there is failure to truly identify Him. Efforts are made to define God and to offer proofs for His existence. In his book WHY I BELIEVE, Dr. D. James Kennedy has demonstrated such efforts. Most astronomers, he says, believe in God as did most scientists of the past. There appears to be a definite movement among scientists today to assert a belief in God. Much proof of design in the cosmos and our world supports this view. Great order is seen everywhere.

The Bible offers the greatest proofs of God's existence, although no formal effort is made to do so; instead, the Bible assumes God's existence: " In the beginning God created the heavens and the earth." (Gen 1:1)

Someone has proposed the following definition of God, based on Scripture: "God is an eternal Personal Being of absolute knowledge, power and goodness." Much testimony exists to support this.

There are three general proofs for God's existence. As already stated, there is the testimony of nations. They all agree. There is the testimony of nature: "The heavens declare the glories of God and the firmament showeth His handiwork." (Psa 19:1) As divine revelation, the Bible describes the being and character of God.

God is a unity. (Isa. 45:21, 22)
God is a Trinity. (I John 5:7)
God is a Spirit. (John 4:24)
God is eternal. (Psa 90:2)
God is omniscient-all knowledge. (Psa 139)
God is omnipotent-all powerful. (Job 36:5, 26)
God is immutable-unchanging. (Mal 3:6)
God is holy. (I Pet 1:16)
God is truth. (Psa 107:2)
God is just. (Psa 89:14)
God is a God of wrath. (Rom. 1:18)
God is good. (Psa 106:1)

The words of Ralston summarize rather conclusively the existence of God:

> The mercy of God is the outgoing of His goodness and love, in manifestation of pity and compassion for such as are in distress or affliction, or are exposed to misery or ruin. Goodness and love look down upon the fallen race, and desire their happiness. Wisdom devises the remedy, pity lets fall her tears of sympathy, and mercy comes to the rescue. But while the guilty turn with indifference or scorn from all the offers of grace, tendered by the hand of mercy, long suffering waits with enduring patience, reiterates the pleadings of mercy, crying 'Why will ye die?' till goodness and love, and pity, and mercy, and long-suffering, having all made their appeals only to be rejected and set at naught, join with justice and holiness, and every perfection of God, in pronouncing upon the incorrigible their fearful and irrevocable doom.

It is imperative that we believe in God!

DO YOU KNOW THAT YOU WILL FACE JUDGMENT?
Hebrews 9:27

The Bible says in the above verse, "It is appointed unto man once to die, but after that the judgment." Paul tells us, as recorded in Acts 17:31, "Because He (God) hath appointed a day in which He will judge the world in righteousness by that man (Jesus), whom He hath ordained." In view of this, Paul says: "God now commandeth all men everywhere to repent." (Acts 17:30) Again, Paul tells us that there will be "the day when God shall judge the secrets of men by Jesus Christ according to my gospel." (Rom 2:16) Some people do not believe in a final judgment; however, the Scriptures above point to a special day for the judgment.Christians will face judgment, also. "We must all appear before the judgment seat of Christ." (Rom 14:10) This judgment for Christians is not a judgment for sin because Jesus bore that judgment for us on the cross. Instead, it will be a judgment for how well we have lived our lives and how well we have served God.

The judgment for sinners will take place at the judgment bar of God. We read in Eccles 12:14 that "God shall bring every work into judgment, with every secret thing, whether it be good, or whether it be evil."In Heb 6:1, 2, we are told that one of the first principles of the gospel is judgment. In fact, all of creation will be subject to judgment. "But the heavens and the earth, which are now, by the same word are kept in store, reserved unto fire against the day of judgment."(2 Pet 3:7)Many warnings can be found in the Scriptures regarding the certainty of the judgment. This is true in both the Old and New Testaments. In Rev 20:ll-15, we get a picture of the Great White Throne Judgment. Here all the dead will be resurrected to stand before God. At that time, books containing the records of the lives people have lived will be opened, and judgment will take place. The voice of man's conscience will be revealed at that time.The fact of judgment is reasonable. This is because God is holy. "In Him is no darkness." Judgment is the inevitable consequence of sin. Sin is not adequately punished in this life, but it will be at the judgment.What is the procedure for judgment? We are told that all nations and all men, "small and great," will appear there, and they will be judged "according to their works." (Rev 20:12) "For we must all appear before the judgment seat of Christ; that everyone may receive the things done in his body, according to that he hath done, whether it be good or bad." (2 Cor 5:10) The judgment, therefore, is a great day of giving account. For thoughts, (I Cor 4:5) "God shall bring every work into judgment, with every secret thing, whether it be good, or whether it be evil." (Eccles 12:14) This will include all secrets of adultery in thought and deed, as well as secret thoughts of harm to our neighbor.

We will give account for the words that we speak. "Every idle word that man shall speak, they shall give an account for in the day of judgment." (Matt 12:36) This will include, not only idle words, but also gossip, falsehoods and lies. David says, "There is not a word in my tongue, but, lo, O Lord, thou knowest it altogether." (Psa 139:4

Cursing and swearing will not escape judgment. Cursing is very popular and often done in ignorance but will be brought into judgment. In fact, conversation in general will be included. (Matt 12:36)

Judgment will be given for all things ungodly. "The Lord cometh to execute judgment upon all, and to convince all that are ungodly among them of all their ungodly deeds which have been ungodly committed, and of all their hard speeches which ungodly sinners have spoken against Him." (Jude l5)

At the judgment, men will give an account for all "deeds done in the body." In fact, David tells us in Psalm 139 that God is everywhere and knows all things." (Verses 7-15) We shall give an account for our relationship to our neighbors. We are motivated to "love our neighbors as ourselves." We will be tested as to how we have done this.

We are warned not to hate our brother. If so, we are like murderers. (I John 3:15) We are told to be reconciled to our neighbor before we come before God and ask for mercy. (Matt 5:24) We are not to harshly judge our neighbor. Jesus said to cast out the beam in our own eye before we judge the mote in our brother's eye. (Matt 7:15) Thus, all of life will be included and laid bare at the judgment. Let us pray that the blood of Jesus will wash our sins away.

At the final day, Christians will be acknowledged, but the wicked will be condemned. (Matt 25:31-46) Do you want to be acknowledged? If so, confess your sins, repent of them, and accept Christ as your Savior. If not, you will hear those terrible words from Jesus: "Depart from me ye workers of iniquity."

"And the books were opened and another book was opened, which is the book of life and whosoever was not found written in the book of life was cast into the Lake of Fire." It is imperative that we all face judgment. God grant that we will do so only in Christ Jesus our Savior.

DO YOU KNOW THAT WE ARE ALL ACCOUNTABLE TO GOD?
Rom 14:12

This Scripture says that "Everyone of us shall give account of himself to God." Here is described another divine imperative. On one occasion, Daniel Webster was asked what his greatest thought was. He replied by saying, "The greatness of God and my accountability to Him." Jesus taught by using parables. In Matt 5:14-30, He gives the parable of the talents. In so doing, He taught that we will give an account for our work and life on earth. Our accountability to God is a fact. "Everyone of us shall give account to God." (Rom 14:12) Again, "We shall all stand before the judgment seat of Christ." (Rom 14:10). We shall give an account for all of life, the use of time, talents, and possessions. Life is a sacred trust from God, and we will be required to make a report on how well we have lived.

Why is this so? Because God is the Creator of life. "None of us liveth to himself and none dieth to himself, for whether we live, we live unto the Lord; whether we die, we die unto the Lord: whether we live therefore or die, we are the Lord's." (Rom 14:7, 8) The Lord is the Sustainer of life, and we are responsible to Him. When Christ returns, we shall stand before Him for a great check-up.

For what are we accountable to God?

For our spiritual condition—first, we must have a transformation and then a consecration to God. Like Paul, "I have a stewardship."

For our life—we should give God full-time Christian service, or secular work, all consecrated to God. "In all thy ways acknowledge Him." (Prov 3:9)

For our talents—we must use them for God's glory. It is sinful to withhold anything from Him. For our possessions—we are to seek first the Kingdom of God; then He will supply our needs.

For our service to God—we have a part in God's service. We are to devote ourselves fully to Him The story is told of an Indian who went to the altar to pray. He said first, "Indian give beads," but there was no satisfaction. Again, he prayed, "Indian give blanket." Still, no satisfaction. Finally, he prayed, "Indian give beads, give blanket, but now Indian gives self." That is the secret!

HAVE YOU REPENTED OF YOUR SINS?
Luke 13:3

Jesus said, "Except ye repent ye shall likewise perish." This is no new message. The prophets of old challenged people to repent. John the Baptist preached, "Repent ye for the kingdom of heaven is at hand." (Matt 3:2) The disciples went out and "commandeth all men everywhere to repent." (Acts 17:30) Repentance is the direct command of God. If it is so important, we must know what it is.

First, let us look at what repentance is not. It is not making good resolutions. Resolutions are no stronger than one's will. It is not fear alone. Felix, the king, was afraid when he heard Paul testify about God, but he did not repent, even though he believed. The devils believe, but they also tremble.

Repentance is not merely feeling better, feeling sorry, grief or regret. We read that "the sorrow of the world bringeth death." (2 Cor 7:10) It is not merely feeling remorse of conscience. Judas experienced that when he betrayed Christ, but he went out and hanged himself. Repentance is not being religious during times of sickness, calamity or death. It is not going to the church altar to weep until we feel better. It is not doing good to relieve the conscience. It is not reformation, nor merely forsaking sin, or joining the church and being baptized. Instead, it involves a genuine hatred for sin. It is not conviction only, but that may lead one to repentance. That is the work of the Holy Spirit.

Repentance is not the admission of guilt for fear of exposure. Balaam was exposed for his love of money, but he did not repent. Achan was exposed for his sin of disobedience, but he, too, did not repent. King Saul confessed his sin to the prophet Samuel, but he did not repent.

If repentance is not any of the above, what is it? First, it is an utter renunciation of sin. Because we hate it and confess it, it involves a definite change of mind regarding sin.

It also involves sorrow "toward" God. We must feel like David who said, "Against thee, thee only, have I sinned." (Psa 51:4) Thus, it involves a forsaking of sin, a genuine sorrow for what we have done. It is sorrow toward God because we have broken His commandments. It is a sense of spiritual heart-brokenness. We have broken God's heart, and this also involves quitting the sin business.

Repentance involves making restitution for what we have done, as far as possible. We are told that the Prodigal Son came to himself, saw the folly of his ways, and realized that he was a sinner. He hated the road he took, condemned it, and went back to his father. He offered to make up, that is make restitution to his father, for what he had done. (Luke 15) The writer remembers that, as a boy, he stole a piece of candy from a store. Later on, when faced with the need of salvation, he sent ten cents to the owner of the store; he made restitution. But some people are not willing to do this. The story is told of a farmer who in secret killed a neighbor's pig. Later, he went to his neighbor, confessed his act, and offered to pay for the pig. His neighbor forgave him.

Repentance involves not only a turning away from sin, but it is also a turning "to" God, surrendering to Him. If we do, we have this promise: "Let the wicked forsake his way, and the unrighteous man his thoughts; and let him return unto the Lord, and He will have mercy upon him; and to our God, for He will abundantly pardon."(Isa 55:7) "God is not willing that any should perish, but that all come to repentance." (2 Pet 3:9) Repentance is a privilege and blessing in this life. One must not wait for the future to do it. "Now is the day of salvation." By so doing, we will be able to successfully meet the judgment of God.

Repentance comes to us by the grace of God. Let us pray the prayer of repentance: "God be merciful to me a sinner." Then by faith receive Jesus Christ as our Saviour and Lord.

In 2 Cor 7:10-11, Paul tells us that godly sorrow will result in certain fruit in our lives; it makes us live more carefully; it clears us of all guilt, fear and condemnation and gives us a desire to serve Him faithfully.

WHAT MUST I DO TO BE SAVED?
Acts 16:30

On the Apostle Paul's second missionary journey, he stopped at a place called Philippi. While there, he was instrumental in the conversion of a woman named Lydia who was a very popular person. (Acts 16:14,15)

While at Philippi, Paul freed a damsel from an evil spirit. (Acts 16:16) As a result, he and Silas were cast into prison. (Acts 16:24) While there, they praised God, and He caused an earthquake to free them. The jailor was afraid that if they escaped he would forfeit his life according to Roman law. In great fear he sought to commit suicide, but Paul prevented this. As a result, the jailor asked Paul the question, "Sirs, what must I do to be saved?" (Vs. 30) The answer Paul gave him resulted in his salvation and that of his family.

Let us analyze this situation. First, this is a practical question. Many people ask what to do to become wealthy, to become beautiful, or to become popular, etc. But the question of salvation is far more important. It is also one that is on the hearts of many people.

This question is a personal one. The jailor was interested first in himself. No one else can ask that question for us either. This was a painful question. The jailor was in agony when he asked it. David asked a similar question in the midst of his troubles. The same is true of other Bible characters. This was also a promising question. It is a hopeful sign when people are concerned about and ask questions concerning salvation. This was a pointed question, a very definite one which deserves a straight answer. The answer to this question concerns salvation. It is a simple matter to find its answer. Let us analyze the question further. What must "I" do to be saved? Who is the I? He is a lost man enslaved by sin, self and Satan. He is a blind man, blinded by Satan to his sin on the one hand and to the Christian life on the other. He is a dead man, cut off from spiritual life to be found only in God.

Again, "What must I do to be "saved?" This is not to be reformed, repaired, or refurbished, but to be redeemed. How can a slave find freedom? How can a blind man find sight? How can a dead man find life?

What must I "do" to be saved? What can a slave do to free himself? What can a blind man do to gain sight? What can a dead man do to make himself alive?

Men have sought to find the answer to the question of salvation in many different ways, but they fail.

Some try to gain salvation by good character, by their own goodness, given time and opportunity. They make the mistake here of measuring themselves with others. But we read, "There is none righteous, no, not one." (Rom 3:10) "For the wrath of God is revealed from heaven against all ungodliness and unrighteousness of men, who hold the truth in unrighteousness," (Rom 1:18) "If we say that we have not sinned, we make Him a liar, and His word is not in us." (I John 1:10) Salvation cannot be found in morality.

Others try to secure salvation through education, but more is required. Education is only a fragment of our responsibility. It is more important to "be" something than it is to know something.

Still others try to find salvation through the performance of good works. While one looks for salvation by character, by what he is, another looks for salvation by education, by what he knows; another looks to service, by what he does. "Can the Ethiopian change his skin, or the leopard his spots? Then ye also do good who are accustomed to do evil." (Jer. 13:23) There is the Old Testament illustration in this regard concerning Cain and Abel. Cain sought God's approval by offering the fruit of "his" labors, but he failed to obtain it. "It is not by works of righteousness which we have done, but according to His mercy He saved us by the washing of regeneration, and renewing of the Holy Spirit." (Tit 3:5)

Still others seek salvation through religion. It is quite true that men are naturally religious, but the natural man cannot please God. (Rom 8:6,7)All of these efforts fall short of securing salvation. What, then, must one do to obtain the salvation so freely provided to man by God?First, the unsaved person must recognize that he is a sinner, and, as long as he remains in this condition, he is separated from God and lost. But there is good news. Luke tells us that "Jesus came to seek and to save the lost." (Luke 19:10)

Second, one must recognize that it is Jesus alone Who can save us. Paul tells us, "Neither is there salvation in any other, for there is none other name under heaven given among men, whereby we must be saved." (Acts 4:12) Third, the sinner must recognize that his sins keep him from being saved. "Behold, the Lord's hand is not shortened, that it cannot save; neither is his ear heavy that it cannot hear, but your iniquities have separated between you and your God, and your sins have hid his face from you." (Isa 59:1)

Fourth, remove sin so that you can be saved. This is done by confessing it. "If we confess our sins, He is faithful and just to forgive us our sins, and to cleanse us from all unrighteousness." (I John 1:9) We are also to forsake sin. " He that covereth his sins shall not prosper; but whoso confesseth and forsaketh them shall have mercy." (Prov 28:13) This means to quit the sinning business. Then, one is able to receive (take) Jesus as Savior. "As many as receive him, to them gave he the power to become sons of God." (John 1:12) Paul told the Philippian jailor, "Believe (have faith) on the Lord Jesus Christ and thou shalt be saved." (Acts 16:31)

In the light of all this, the challenge comes to the sinner—what will you do about it? If one is sick, he calls the doctor; Jesus is the Great Physician. If the criminal is in jail, he calls a lawyer. The sinner is criminal before God. Jesus Christ is the great Lawgiver. "If any man sins, we have an advocate with the Father, Jesus Christ the righteous, and he is the propitiation for sins; and not for ours only but also for the sins of the whole world." (I John 2:2)

At the wedding the bride says, "I do take him," thus making a covenant with her husband. Likewise, the sinner must make a covenant with God and quit sinning; then "I do take (receive) Jesus as my Savior."Don't put it off. "Boast not thyself of tomorrow, for thou knowest not what a day may bring forth." (Prov 27:1)

If one knows he is a sinner, if he believes Christ died for us, if he is willing to confess and repent and forsake sin, and if he is willing to believe, then come to Jesus at this moment. We have the promise of Jesus, "Whosoever therefore shall confess me before men, him will I also confess before my Father in heaven, but whosoever shall deny me before men, him will I also deny before my Father Who is in heaven." (Matt 10:32)

WHAT WILL YOU DO WITH CHRIST?
Matt 27:22

During his last hours on earth, Jesus faced Pontius Pilate. The Jews had falsely accused Jesus of crimes He did not commit, so He faced judgment at the hands of Pilate who sought to free Him. Failing to do so, Pilate asked the question, "What shall I do then with Jesus which is called Christ?" (Matt 27:22)This is a question proposed to us. It is a most important question because the answer we give to it determines our destiny. We cannot be indifferent to this matter. We cannot be on the fence to it. It is a question which concerns each soul because "We shall all stand before the judgment of Christ." (Rom 14:10)

If our answer is right, then we will enjoy eternal life. If we answer wrongly, we will suffer eternal loss.

What depends on what we do with Jesus? First, our acceptance or rejection before God is determined. "He that believeth on Him (Jesus) is not condemned, but he that believeth not is condemned already because he hath not believed in the name of the only begotten Son of God." (John 3:18) Our acceptance with God depends directly on our acceptance of Jesus Christ. "Be it known unto you therefore, men and brethren, that through this man (Jesus) is preached unto you forgiveness of sins: and by Him all that believe are justified from all things from which ye could not be justified by the law of Moses." (Acts 13:38, 39)

Second, the answer to this question will determine our becoming sons of God or children of the devil. "As many as received Him (Jesus) to them gave He power to become sons of God, even to them that believe on His name." (John 1:12)Third, our having peace or not depends on how we answer this question. "Therefore being justified by faith we have peace with God through our Lord Jesus Christ." (Rom 5:1) Through Jesus we have peace "with" God and "of" God. Rejection brings distress and despair.

Fourth, the answer to this question determines whether or not we have eternal life. "He that believeth on the Son hath everlasting life, and he that believeth not shall not see life; but the wrath of God abideth on him." (John 3:36)What "must" we do with Christ? This question stands before us. We must either accept or reject Him. The chief priests and elders rejected Jesus. The crowd said, "Crucify Him." Will we stand with the crowd, or will we accept Him? The friends, disciples and others accepted Him. Are you?

Pilate was faced with a decision. He tried to take the middle ground, but there was none. He was swayed by the people. Are you? The religious leaders of that day professed a belief in the Messiah, but they did not accept Jesus.

We must let Jesus into our hearts or shut Him out. Jesus said, "I stand at the door and knock; if any man will hear my voice, and open the door, I will come in to him, and will sup with him, and he with me." (Rev 3:20) We can choose to close our hearts. God can't even open them. We must do one or the other.We must confess or deny Jesus. He said, "Whosoever therefore will confess me before men, him will I confess before my Father which is in heaven. But whosoever shall deny me before men, him will I also deny before my Father which is in heaven." (Matt 10:32, 33) Our denial brings His denial.

We must take our stand for or against Jesus. He said, "He that is not with me is against me." (Matt 12:30) There is no middle ground to take.

What are the results of our attitude toward Jesus? If we reject, deny, or take the middle ground, we must remember that "God hath made Jesus whom ye have crucified, both Lord and Christ." (Acts

2:36) "Wherefore God also hath highly exalted him, and given him a name which is above every name; that at the name of Jesus every knee should bow and every tongue should confess that Jesus Christ is Lord." (Phil 2:9-11) Jesus will judge us by His Word at the final judgment.

The story is told of a judge whose friend appeared in court before him. The judge pronounced a negative judgment on his friend. "But, Judge," the friend responded, "you are my friend." To which the judge replied, "Then I was your friend; now I am your judge."There is great reward for us if we accept Jesus as Savior and Lord. "He was wounded for our transgressions and was bruised for our iniquities; the chastisement of our peace was upon him; and with his stripes we are healed; all we like sheep have gone astray; we have turned everyone to his own way; and the Lord hath laid on Him the iniquity of us all." (Isa 53:5, 6) "Behold, what manner of love the Father hath bestowed upon us, that we should be called the sons of God—beloved, now are we sons of God." (I John 3:1-3). Think of the joys that lie ahead!

WHAT SHALL YOU DO TO INHERIT ETERNAL LIFE?
Mark 10:17

On one occasion a young man approached Jesus and asked Him this question: "Good Master, what shall I do to inherit eternal life?" (Mark 10:17) This is a very important question, the answer to which involves one of God's divine imperatives.

We live in a world full of death. Everywhere there are ravages of war, disease, famine, traffic accidents, etc., all of which result in death. Also, in view of the spiritual death of the sinner, the answer to this is important.

All of us face an impending death. The Scriptures tell us: "It is appointed unto man once to die, but after this the judgment." (Heb 9:27) In view of the life to come, the answer to this question is important.

The question of eternal life became of great interest to the young man who approached Jesus. (Mark 10:17-31) He was a rich, young ruler. In the final analysis, as the story goes, this young man was too devoted to riches and other things. He deemed riches and great possessions as more important. He indicated that he had kept the commandments. It is apparent that he was satisfied with his own goodness.

Jesus informed him that God was the only source of goodness and eternal life. (Mark 10:18) Material possessions are superficial and transient.

The boy's religion was not enough. He had kept the commandments. (Mark 10:19) He had lived a commendable life and had done many worthy things, but this did not touch what he was. God is more interested in what we are than what we do. "It is not by works of righteousness which we have done, but according to His mercy He saved us, by the washing of regeneration, and renewing of the Holy Ghost." (Titus 3:5-7)

The answer to the question of eternal life is not to be found in a religion of morality. (Mark 10:20) Jesus loved the young man because he was so close to the kingdom. (Mark10:21) He had such marvelous possibilities like so many people today. There are hosts of so-called "good people," good-hearted people, but they, like the young ruler, lack something important.

In Verse 21 we are told that the young man had great possessions which became his god. So it is with people today. Great possessions can prove to be a stumbling block to people if they give them the highest priority in their lives. Rather, it is better to lay up treasures in heaven, than on earth. (Matt 6:20, 21)

This story reveals the weakness of the rich, young ruler. His underlying cause was sin. He had a carnal mind, which means the minding of the flesh. (Rom 8:6-8)How, then, can one obtain eternal life? Jesus gave the answer to the young man. Get rid of earthly treasures, and turn away from the things we love more than we love God. (Mark 10:21) This is the way to eternal life.We are to come to Christ, take up our cross, which means death to sin and self, and follow Him. (Mark 10:21) Then we will be in a position to serve. But the young man was not willing to pay the price and went away sorrowful. (Mark 10:22)In Mark 10:21 and 30, Jesus pointed out that those who are willing to pay the price and put God first in their hearts and lives will have their needs met, and, in the world to come, eternal life.

HAVE YOU BEEN CONVERTED?
Matt 18:1-6

Most people would confess that they have a desire to go to heaven. Jesus Christ dealt with this subject in Matt 18:1-6 when He said, "Except ye be converted and become as little children, ye shall not enter the kingdom of heaven." The word "except" here indicates conversion as one of the divine imperatives.

What does it mean to be converted? The word itself means to turn about, to turn around. A Biblical illustration of the spiritual meaning of conversion is given in the experience of the Apostle Paul on the road to Damascus. Paul intended to go to Damascus to persecute the Christians, but God met Paul on the road and completely reversed his plans and life. Paul was converted there and became a stalwart advocate of Christianity. Another good illustration is that of the young man called the Prodigal Son. (Lk 15:11-15) The record here shows that this boy turned his back on his father and wasted his life in sin. He later "came to himself" and turned back to his father who forgave him.

As a divine imperative, the sinner needs to turn away from sin and turn to God. In fact, conversion is a requirement for everyone if he expects to get to heaven. "Repent ye, and be converted, that your sins may be blotted out." (Acts 3:19) Repentance is the inner aspect of conversion. There is also the outward aspect of turning aside from sin. Not only is conversion a requirement to qualify us for heaven, but the needs of men also demand it. First, sin has led man in the wrong direction, away from God. Gen. 6:3 says, " In their going astray, they are become flesh."

There are only two ways or roads for us to travel. "Enter ye in at the strait gate: for wide is the gate, and broad is the way, that leadeth to destruction, and many there be that go in thereat, because strait is the gate, and narrow is the way, which leadeth unto life, and few that be that find it." (Matt 7:13, 14) Thus, sin leads man along the road to hell. To avoid this, conversion is necessary.

Second, sin has separated man from God. "The Lord's hand is not shortened that it cannot save, neither is his ear heavy that it cannot hear, but your iniquities have separated between you and your God and your sins have hid his face from you." (Isa 59:1, 2) Therefore the sinner is admonished to "turn ye, turn ye." "Come out from among them and be ye separate saith the Lord, and I will receive you." (2 Cor 6:17,18)

Third, conversion is imperative because Satan has blinded men and led them along the wrong path. "The god of this world (Satan) has blinded the minds of them that believe not, lest the light of the glorious gospel of Christ, who is the image of God, should shine into them." (2 Cor 4:4)

Fourth, conversion is necessary because the way of the ungodly shall perish. (Psa 1:6) Salvation depends on conversion.Fifth, conversion is required because men walk in a way of error. Men may think they walk correctly, but sin leads them in the way of error. This is because the very nature of sin is to deceive, delude blind men, and allure them away from God.Sixth, conversion is imperative because to live in sin is man's way to hell. "The wicked shall be turned into hell, and all nations that forget God." (Psa 9:17)How is one converted? Repentance is necessary. This means to be genuinely sorry for what we have done. Conversion means to quit the sinning business, to turn our way around from it and turn to God. "Commit thy way unto the Lord: trust also in him; and he shall bring it to pass." (Psa 37:5) The secret to conversion, therefore, involves repentance, commitment to God, and trusting him for forgiveness. This results in a new direction, a new way to go, a new heart, and a new life.

Not only does conversion qualify us to become God's children, it also qualifies and prepares us for Christian service. (Luke 22:32)In the light of all that has been said above, it becomes evident, therefore, that conversion of humanity becomes the supreme task of the church. (James 5:19) The quality of the converted life, says Jesus, is to "become as little children." A child depends on his father, trusts his father, loves his father, obeys his father, seeks to please his father, and lives humbly in the sight of God." (Matt. 18:4) All of these things are characteristic of one who has been converted.

HAVE YOU BEEN BORN AGAIN?
John 3:1-8

A man by the name of Nicodemus came to Jesus at night. Who was he? A Pharisee, a ruler of the Jews. (John 3:1-15) He recognized Jesus as a great teacher and worker of miracles. Jesus told him that he must be born again to enter heaven, but Nicodemus did not understand His meaning, thinking that Jesus referred to a physical birth. (Vs. 4) Jesus taught him that a spiritual birth was required. (Vs. 5) The same is true for so many people today, for they do not know the true meaning of the new birth.

A study of this passage of Scripture shows three elements of this divine imperative:
    1. The Necessity of the New Birth Expressed
    2. The Nature of the New Birth Explained
    3. The Possibility of the New Birth Experienced

First, Jesus told Nicodemus that the new birth was <u>necessary</u> to enter the Kingdom of God. "Ye cannot see," (Vs. 3) "Ye cannot enter," (Vs. 5) and "Ye must." (Vs. 7) To get into the spiritual realm, it is necessary to be born into it.

The great preacher Spurgeon was asked, "Why do you preach so much on the new birth?" He replied, "Ye must" be born again.

Because there is much confusion on what the new birth is, we will look first at what it is not. First, the new birth is not <u>generation</u> or physical birth. Jesus told Nicodemus that physical birth was one thing, but spiritual birth was another. (Vs. 6) The new birth is not inheritable; it is not the result of "blue blood." The Apostle John put it this way: the sons of God are "born, not of blood, nor of the will of the flesh, nor of the will of man, but of God." (John 1:13) As a Pharisee, Nicodemus had to be a good man to reach his position as a member of the ruling body, the Sanhedrin, but this did not make him automatically qualified for the new birth.

Second, the new birth is not <u>education</u>. It is not mere cultivation, information, teaching or training. One may train lions to perform acts, but they will fight in the cage just the same. One may even know the Bible yet not be born again. By knowing the Bible, someone has said, "You may have heaven in your head but hell in your soul."

Third, the new birth is not <u>cultivation</u>. It is not the refinement found in so many churches. Some years ago the writer watched a man dress a pig. At various stages of adding dress, he would hold the pig up and say, "Is it still a pig?" No amount of clothes changed the pig's nature.

Fourth, the new birth is not <u>confirmation</u>. One may even be baptized, join the church and still not be born again. An individual once asserted, "If baptism would save us, then we can be knocked in the head and held under the water until we go to heaven." The Apostle Paul stated, "In Christ Jesus neither circumcision nor uncircumcision availed anything, but a new creation." (Gal 6:15) Nicodemus fasted and prayed, but that was not enough.

Great knowledge is not enough. "The world by wisdom knew not God." (I Cor 1:21)

Fifth, the new birth is not <u>natural goodness</u>. Nicodemus was a good man but was not born again. "There is a way which seemeth right unto a man, but the ends thereof are the ways of death." (Prov 14:12)

Sixth, the new birth is not <u>good works</u>. Nicodemus had done good things for people and the poor, but this was not the new birth. "Not by works of righteousness which we have done, but according to his mercy he saved us." (Titus 3:5) "For by grace are ye saved— not of works." (Eph 2:8)

Seventh, the new birth is not merely being <u>religious</u>. Nicodemus was that, but he did not qualify.

If for these and other reasons the new birth is not possible, what, then, is it? It comes by way of a divine change in man's heart. "As many as received him(Jesus), to them gave he power to become the sons of God." (John 1:12) Thus, we see the nature of the new birth explained.

It is a complete change. "If any man be in Christ, he is a new creation." (2 Cor 5:17)

It is a spiritual change. Jesus told Nicodemus he had to be born of the Spirit. (John 3:5, 6) "It is not by works of righteousness which we have done—but by the washing of regeneration and the renewal of the Holy Spirit." (Titus 3:3-5)

It is a supernatural change. Jesus likened it to the wind, which we cannot see, but we can feel. (John 3:8) It is the impartation of divine life. (2 Peter 1:4)

It has to be a permanent change. We have everlasting life. There must be no more sinning. One must stay in the Christian way.

This passage shows us the possibility of the new birth <u>experienced</u>. That very familiar passage of John 3:16 shows that God gave His Son that we might, through the new birth, have everlasting life.

Why do we need the new birth? Our nature requires it. As a sinner we are unfit for God's presence. Through Adam's sin, man has inherited a sinful nature, and this has to be changed before we can be acceptable to God.

God's nature requires it. God cannot and will not countenance sin, for He is holy. The new birth enables us to partake of the divine nature. (2 Peter 1:4)

The work of Christ requires it. If there were some other way to be saved, Christ would not have died. Jesus said, "I am the way." "Without the shedding of blood there is no remission of sin." (Heb 9:22)

The Word of God requires it. Jesus said, "Ye must." Peter said a person is born again, not of corruptible seed, but, of incorruptible, by the Word of God." (I Peter 1:23)

What does the new birth do for us? It takes care of the past. Through pardon and forgiveness, our sins are blotted out. It will take care of the present. Jesus is our constant companion, as our

Savior, Guide and Provider. We need not be afraid when Jesus is with us. It takes care of the future since the new birth qualifies us for a place in heaven. Jesus said, "In my Father's house are many mansions." (John 14:2)

How does one obtain the new birth? Jesus told Nicodemus that the working of the Holy Spirit in man's heart is really a mystery. We know that He is present, but how He works is not known. It is like the wind. We are born of God.

The new birth takes place in us when we repent of our sins, confess our need of Jesus as Savior, and receive Him into our hearts by faith. (John 1:12,14-16) We are all children of God by faith. (Gal 3:26)

What are the results of the new birth? We become new creatures in Christ Jesus, by receiving life from above. (Gal 2:20) We become more like God. (Eph 4:24) We have victory over sin (I John 5:4) and begin to live righteously. (I John 2:29) We have a new heart, a new motivation, new life, and a new destination. (John 3:36)

IS JESUS CHRIST FIRST IN YOUR LIFE?
Col 1:18

In writing to the Colossian Church, the Apostle Paul asserted that Jesus Christ was to have first place in their lives and in all things. "That in all things He might have the preeminence." (Col 1:18) This simply means that Jesus Christ has first place because God the Father gave it to Him.

First, the preeminence of Christ is seen in relation to Himself. "Who is the image of the invisible God, the first born of every creature?" (Col 1:15) The writer to the Hebrews spoke of Jesus as God's spokesman, God's image and the Creator and Administrator of the universe. (Heb 1:1-4)

Men have tried to reduce Jesus, to make Him mere man, a prophet, a seer, and a good example. God said, however, that "it pleased the Father that in Him should all fullness dwell." (Col 1:19) Likewise, the Apostle Paul said, "For the Father judgeth no man, but hath committeth all judgment unto the Son: that all men should honor the Son, even as they honor the Father. He that honoreth not the Son honoreth not the Father which hath sent Him." (John 5:22, 23)

Second, Jesus was preeminent in the creation. "For by Him were all things created, that are in heaven and that are in earth." (Col 1:16) The writer to the Hebrews tells us that "he upholds all things by the word of his power." (Heb 1:3) It is thus that we have cosmos, not chaos.

Third, Christ is preeminent in the church. "And He is the head of the body, the church." (Col 1:18) The secret of the church's success is the exaltation of Christ. If this is not so, ecclesiasticism reigns, and there is a loss of passion and evangelism. Any attack on the deity of Christ, as we see in some circles, points up a real problem for the church.

Fourth, Christ is preeminent in the plan of salvation and redemption. There is proof of this by what He has done: "Who hath delivered us from the power of darkness—in whom we have redemption through his blood, even the forgiveness of our sins." (Col 1:13,14) He has "made peace through the blood of his cross, by him to reconcile all things unto himself." (Col 1:20, 21) Thus, Christ made a provision for peace and reconciliation with God as well as holiness of heart and life.

The method by which Jesus accomplished this was to bring about an inward change in the heart of the sinner "which is Christ 'in' you." (Col 1:27) This was done through a quickening of the Spirit of man from the dead to new spiritual life. (Col 2:13,14)

Why did Christ do this? His motive was to "present you holy and unblameable and unreprovable in his sight," (Col 1:22) to provide great spiritual riches to the believer, (Col 1:27) and to present the believer "perfect in Christ Jesus." (Col 1:27, 28)

Fifth, Christ will be preeminent when He comes again. "Wherefore God hath highly exalted him, and given him a name which is above every name: that at the name of Jesus every knee should bow, of things in heaven, and things in earth, and things under the earth; and that every tongue should confess that Jesus Christ is Lord." (Phil 2:9-11) The means and methods by which Jesus will do these things is vividly described for us in Rev 19:18-21; 20:11-15.

Because Jesus is preeminent in all things, He deserves and desires first place now: in our thinking, in our hearts, in our lives, in our homes, churches and schools. "That Christ may dwell in your hearts by faith," (Eph 3:17) and in our nation and the world. (Col 1:16)

Thus, the preeminence of Christ in us personally is a divine imperative.

ARE YOU READY FOR THE SECOND COMING OF CHRIST?
Luke 21:5-7, 25-28, 36

All Christians should study prophecy. Most of the Bible is devoted to this subject. There is one particular aspect of prophecy that we will stress here—the Second Coming of Christ.

As one reads the Scripture, it is to be noted that a state of readiness for the second coming of Christ is recommended. Scripture reveals three conditions in which a state of readiness is demanded:

1. Watchfulness
2. Prayerfulness
3. Worthiness

First, Jesus said, "Watch ye therefore." There is Scriptural emphasis on watchfulness. Further, Jesus said, "Take heed" (Luke 21:8) and "when ye see these things." (Luke 21:31)

The word "watch" is used sixty-one times in the Old Testament and thirty times in the New Testament. "Take heed" is mentioned eighty times in the Old Testament and thirty times in the New Testament. Again, Jesus said, "Be not deceived." (Luke 21:8) This demands watchfulness.

The Scriptures provide us with directions on watchfulness. In Luke 21:34, Jesus said for us to watch ourselves by saying, "Take heed to yourselves." The Apostle Paul gave much the same advice:

"Seeing then that all these things shall be dissolved, what manner of persons ought ye to be in all holy conversation (living) and godliness." (2 Peter 3:11) He said again, "Wherefore, beloved, seeing that ye look for such things, be diligent that ye may be found of him in peace, without spot, and blameless." (2 Peter 3:14) The record of our lives should be clean so that there will be no basis for accusation against us.

To be ready, purity of heart is necessary. "And now, little children, abide in him; that, when he shall appear, we may have confidence, and not be ashamed before him at his coming." (I John 2:28) This demands watchfulness. Again, John tells us that the hope of the second coming should motivate us to be pure. (I John 3:3) This demands watchfulness. The Apostle Peter continues this emphasis when he advised Christians to be holy. (I Peter 1:16) Titus does the same. (Titus 2:11-14)

Christians are instructed on proper attitudes to be manifested in connection with the second coming:

> Sobriety—"Let us watch and be sober." (I Thess 5:1-6)
> Patience—"Ye have need of patience—yet a little while—He shall come." (Heb 10:36-37)
> Love for His coming—"A crown of righteousness is given for those who love His Coming." (2 Tim 4:8)
> Faithfulness— Jesus said, "Because iniquity shall abound, the love of many shall wax cold." (Matt 24:12)
> Observation of the Lord's Supper—This is done in remembrance of Him. (Luke 22:19) By so doing, we show The Lord's death till He comes. (I Cor 11:26)

In addition to watching ourselves, we are told to watch our service. The certainty of the second coming should convict us of inactivity. Several Scriptures point out the importance of our service in the light of the second coming:
> We should be faithful and wise servants—Matt 24:42-51.

We should use our talents to serve Him—Matt 25:14-30.
Our service will be revealed when Jesus returns—Matt 25:31-46.
We will be judged by our works—Rev 22:12.
We are to occupy till He comes—Luke 19:13.
With faith fixed on the cross and hope fixed on the second coming, love should issue in service.
There should be particular faithfulness in ministry—2 Tim 4:1, 2; I Peter 5:2-4.
We are told to watch society.
> There is the spirit of restlessness and sin, unrest in the holy land, war, and what is happening to the Jews.

We are to watch the solar system.
> There will be great signs in the heavens—Luke 21:25-28.

There will also be the spirit of expectancy.
> Such a spirit was present at the first coming of Jesus (Luke 2). The same kind of spirit is prevalent among God's people today.

We are to watch particularly for the second coming of Jesus.
> He promised to return—John 14:3.
> The angels promised, also—Acts 1:11.
> Paul said, "The Lord Himself will come"—I Thess 4:16,17.
> He may come at any time—Matt 24:44; Luke 17:24-30.
> We should be ready to be caught up to meet Him-I Thess 4; 2 Tim 4:6-8.

There is a close relationship between watchfulness and prayer, according to scripture. We are to be alert, be in communion with Him and pray for others to be ready. (Matt 28:41; Mark 13:33)

The third condition to be met is that of worthiness. This word can be defined as firmness, tenaciousness, merit, and strength.

These words represent traits to be manifested by those who seek to be worthy of God's approval at the second coming of Christ.

There can be two emphases here: (1) to escape, and (2) to stand. One scripture stresses the need for one to escape the pitfalls of temptation. Luke 21:36 stresses watchfulness and prayerfulness to escape anything that would keep one from being ready for the coming of Jesus. In view of the coming judgment, Paul urges the Thessalonians to obey the gospel to escape the wrath and judgment of God. (2 Thess 1:7-9)

We are not only admonished to escape but also to stand. We must be faithful to stand in his presence, for some day we will do so; however, we are encouraged to know that God has made provision for us to stand before Him through the blood of Christ, in victory. There will be the grand judgment of rewards at the Judgment Seat of Christ. From then on, we will reign with Him forever. Are you ready? This is a divine imperative.

HOW SHALL WE ESCAPE IF WE NEGLECT SO GREAT A SALVATION?
Heb 2:3

"How shall we escape if we neglect so great a salvation?" (Heb 2:3) This is one of the great texts of the Bible which reminds us of another divine imperative. This text denotes three natural divisions: (1) how shall we escape if we neglect salvation? (2) the neglect of it, and (3) a great salvation. We focus on the third division, great salvation.

Notice the little word "so" which takes the meaning out into infinity. "For God so loved the world, that He gave His only begotten Son, that whoever believeth in Him should not perish, but have everlasting life." (John 3:16) Why is salvation so great? Why must, in the light of its greatness, we not neglect it? There are at least three general reasons why salvation is so great: (1) its origination; (2) its manifestation; and (3) its adaptation. First, salvation is great because God is its author. Thus, salvation is great since God is great. God is Creator, Provider, and Administrator of the universe.

God is great in His person. "Lord, thou hast been our dwelling place in all generations. Before the mountains were brought forth, or ever thou hast formed the earth, even from everlasting to everlasting thou art God." (Psa 90:1, 2)

God is great in His presence. In Psalm 139 David spoke of God being everywhere. He is great in His power. "The heavens declare the glories of God, and the firmament showed His handiwork." (Psa 19:1) "He upholds all things by the word of His power." (Heb 1:3) Jesus said, "All power is given unto me in heaven and earth."

God is great in His provision. "My God shall supply all your needs according to His riches in glory." (Phil 4:19)

Second, salvation is great because of its manifestation in Jesus Christ, Son of God. He, too, was great in His Person. "He that hath seen me hath seen the Father." (John 14:9) He is great in His presence. He said, "Lo, I am with you always." He is great in His power. He said, "All power is given unto me in heaven and in earth."

Jesus was great in His provision. He is the light of the world. He is the way, the truth and the life. "He is able to save unto the uttermost all who come unto Him by faith."

Third, salvation is great because of its adaptation to man. Salvation really works for mankind because it works during times of sickness, in times of affliction, in times of approaching death, in times of adversity by giving peace, and in times of the loss of loved ones and close friends.

Salvation is great because it provides full salvation. It not only saves from the guilt of sin, but it also provides a clean heart, a pure heart, and the infilling of the Holy Spirit.

Salvation is great because it provides for our future. It will qualify us to pass the judgment of God in the last days and will provide a future home where there will be no sickness, no sorrow, no pain, no hunger, no weariness, no age, and no death.. There will be perfect peace, joy, love, and victory for evermore.

How shall we escape, if we neglect so great a salvation?

DO YOU KNOW THAT YOU NEED GOD'S HOLINESS?
Heb 12:14

The writer to the Hebrews tells us that without holiness no man shall see the Lord. (Heb 12:14) Here is another one of God's imperatives.

The words "without holiness" define a condition of mankind without God. It is a description of the world with all of its sin and wickedness. The Apostle Paul tells us the "whole world lieth in wickedness." (I John 5:19)

These words also describe each individual without God. Men are unholy in thoughts, in words, and deeds. Jesus said, "Out of the heart proceed evil thoughts, murders, adulteries, fornication, thefts, false witness—these are the things which defile a man." (Matt 15:19, 20) Paul wrote to the Roman church and gave a list of the many sins that men commit. (Rom 1:28-32) Without holiness means "without God," for "God is holy."

Some of the manifestations of being without holiness include:

> One cannot enter heaven. (Rev 21:27)
> One cannot have perfect love. (James 4:17)
> One cannot walk in His ways.
> One cannot keep His commandments.
> One will be prone to wander away from God.

One will love the world in his heart.
One will criticize and be opposed to holiness.

The second thing that we note in Heb 12:14 is "no man shall see the Lord."

In sin, man is spiritually blind. He is blinded by Satan, (2 Cor 4:4) and without holiness he will remain so.

Holiness in us makes it possible for us to see God, to be aware of His presence.

It is an unlawful thing to be shut off from God. (I John 1:6, 7) No evil person will see God. (Eph 5:5)

Without holiness, man manifests all the works of the flesh, (Gal 5:19-21) but "with holiness" we can see God.

The word "no man" implies the kind of holiness man can have. It is not absolute holiness—only God, not man, can have this. We are called to holiness. (I Thess 4:7) What is it? This kind of holiness is a deliverance from sin. (I John 1:7) God has not called us to uncleanness but to holiness. (I Thess 4:7) This is a state of heart and life. How does one obtain holiness?

By separation from all sin (2 Cor 6:17-7:1) This is a separation which leads one to conversion. "Put on the new man, which after God is created in righteousness and true holiness." (Eph 4:24)

By cleansing By putting off all sin (Col 3:8)
By putting on the fruit of the Spirit (Col 3:12)

ARE YOU WALKING IN THE WAY OF HOLINESS
I John1; Isa 35:8

Isaiah tells us, "And a highway shall be there and a way, and it shall be called the way of holiness." (Isa 35:8) It is imperative that we walk in this way.

Scripture reveals that it is the chief purpose of God to bring unto Himself a holy people. He has made provision for us to partake of His own nature—holiness. (Heb 12:10) It is reasonable to conclude that what God requires He will make provision for. This provision is based on God's choice, even from the very beginning. (Eph 1:3,4) God's provision for man's holiness was consummated on the cross by Jesus. By dying for us, Jesus provided "a new and living way." (Heb 10:19, 20)

The atonement by Christ is not limited in its efficacy for sin. It is not limited to outward acts of sin, but the inward bent, called the carnal nature, which is cleansed by the Spirit of God. (I John 1:7; Heb 13:12; Titus 2:14)

God never intended for the heart to be a hiding place for sin and Satan. Some Christians seem to make apology for their carnal nature and attempt to suppress and subjugate it. The excuse is made that they cannot help themselves. Why is it that some people limit God in this matter? Satan is not stronger than God.

The Scriptures plainly teach a cleansing of the inward bent to sin. "If we confess our sins, he is faithful and just to forgive us our sins, and to 'cleanse' us from all unrighteousness." (I John 1:9)

Paul discovered the inward struggle with the carnal nature, but after discovering it, he said, "O wretched man that I am, who shall deliver me from this body of death?" (Rom 7:24) He answered this question by testifying of his own experience. "I thank God through Jesus Christ our Lord." (Rom 7:24) The Bible says, "We are more than conquerors through him that loved us." (Rom 8:37)

This way is one of complete deliverance from all sin. It is the way of the Crucified One. He prayed that His disciples might know the reality of the crucifixion of the self-life. "For their sakes I sanctify myself, that they also might be sanctified through the truth." (John 17:19)

This way of holiness is often opposed because people are not willing to crucify self or to admit their inner struggles.

This way of holiness is necessary. This is why it is one of the divine imperatives. First, because it is commanded. Peter tells us, "Be ye holy." (I Peter 1:16) The Lord Himself said, "For I am the Lord, your God; ye shall therefore sanctify yourselves, and ye shall be holy, for I am holy." (Lev 1:44) God commanded Abraham to "walk before me and be thou perfect." (Gen.17:1) Jesus commanded the disciples, "Be ye therefore perfect, even as your Father in heaven is perfect." (Matt 5:48)

Second, the holy walk is necessary because it is essential. The writer to the Hebrews said, "Follow peace with all men, and holiness without which no man shall see the Lord." (Heb 12:14) The Book of Revelation reveals that "there shall in no wise enter into it(heaven) anything that defileth, neither worketh abomination, or maketh a lie; but they that are written in the Lamb's Book of Life." (Rev 21:27)

The holiness way of life is made possible for us through consecration and faith. In Acts 26:18 we are told that we are "sanctified by faith that is in me." (Jesus) Do you have faith enough to walk in the way of holiness?

DO YOU KNOW HOW TO LIVE A SEPARATED LIFE?
2 Cor 6:17 - 7:1

In writing to the church at Corinth, the Apostle Paul instructed them on how living a separated life would lead to adoption into the family of God. "Come out from among them, and be ye separate, saith the Lord, and touch not the unclean, and I will receive you, and will be a Father unto you, and ye shall be my sons and daughters, saith the Lord Almighty." (2 Cor 6:17)

This reveals to us that God's standard is separation. Men were created for God's use and possession, but sin brought the fall of men into sin and into Satan's use and possession. Separation becomes necessary to restore man to God's fellowship. This is another divine imperative.

We see the idea of separation in God's mind. Paul tells us that Christians were "chosen in Him before the foundation of the world, that we should be holy." (Eph 1:4) When Adam and Eve sinned, God separated Himself from them. He chose Noah and separated him from the rest of the world. He separated Abraham from Ur of Chaldea and sent him into a land that he knew not. He separated Moses and the Israelites and brought them out of Egypt. (Deut 14:2; Lev 20:24, 26)

Thus, they were to be different people. He changed their position and condition. They were to live holy lives. (Lev 20:7, 8)

He separated the prophets from the people in order to give them special ministries.

He separated the church from the world. The ECCLESIA means "called out ones from the world."

Separation is still God's standard. We are called to be saints. (Rom 1:6,7) We are a special people, a holy people. (I Peter 2:9) In Peter's passage, the word "peculiar" means pilgrims and strangers. Thus, God calls us to spiritual "isolation" and spiritual "insulation." In separation, we are to separate from sin unto God.

The need for separation is seen in the condition of the church. The world is so churchy, and the church is so worldly, so separation is demanded.

The need for separation is seen, further, in the attitude of the world toward separation. John 15:19-20 speaks of the hatred of the world toward separation.

The need for separation is seen in the example of Jesus. Heb 9:26 tells us that He was separate from sinners. He said Himself, "I am not of the world." (John 17:16)

The Holy Spirit and the world do not mix. John tells us that "The Spirit of Truth whom the world cannot receive because it seeth him not, neither knoweth him." (John 14:17)

We are admonished by Paul, "Be ye not unequally yoked together with unbelievers, for what fellowship hath righteousness with unrighteousness." (2 Cor 6:14) The Apostle John advises us not to love the world. (I John 2:15-17) James tells us that "the friendship of the world is enmity with God." (James 4:4) A worldly Christian can be compared to an unfaithful spouse. In fact, compromise will not work.

The fact of the matter is that the world expects Christians to be separate. If there is no difference between them, who knows which is which?

The separated life demands separation from sinful world pleasures and worldly alliances. There are unworthy business alliances to be avoided. There are unworthy marriage alliances. Christians are admonished to marry "only in the Lord." (I Cor 7:39)

Christians are to be separate from worldly companions. Fraternizing with sinners dulls one's spirituality. We are to make friends with God's children.

What is the secret to separation? "Having therefore these promises, let us cleanse ourselves from all filthiness of the flesh and spirit, perfecting holiness in the fear of God." (2 Cor 7:1) Thereby we develop a new love, the love of God.

By so doing, we turn from unrighteousness to righteousness. We turn from darkness to light. (I John 1:5, 6) We turn from idols to Christ. (I John 2:15-17)

To accomplish this, one must "come out" and be separate and touch not the unclean thing. (2 Cor 6:17)

If we do this, we have the promise of God the Father that He will become our Father and that we can become His sons and daughters. (2 Cor 6:17,18)

There are great rewards for those who live separated lives. We have the "exceeding great and precious promises whereby we are partakers of the divine nature." (2 Peter1:4) We are cleansed of the flesh and spirit. We are the recipients of the holiness of God. (Rom 12:1)

DO YOU KNOW HOW TO LIVE A CLEAN LIFE?
Eph 4:30; I Thess 5:19

This study is concerned with two commandments found in the Word of God. Wherever a command is found, a divine imperative is involved.

Both of these commandments concern Christians and directly impact a Christian life-style: (1) Do not grieve the Holy Spirit, (Eph. 4:30) and (2) Do not quench the Spirit. (I Thess 5:13)

If a Christian is to live up to the name "saint," all uncleanness must go. The infilling of the Holy Spirit demands a clean heart and life.

The first commandment follows: "Grieve not the Holy Spirit, whereby ye are sealed unto the day of redemption." (Eph 4:30) The word "grieve" is a love word. If we grieve the Holy Spirit, we cause Him pain because He loves us.

What is involved in causing the Divine Spirit grief? He is the Spirit of truth, (John 14:47) so anything false, deceitful or hypocritical gives Him grief.

He is the Spirit of faith. (2 Cor 4:13) Doubt, distrust, worry, or anxiety grieves Him.

He is the Spirit of grace. (Heb 10:29) Whatever is hard, bitter, ungracious, unforgiving, or unloving grieves Him.

He is the Spirit of holiness. (Rom 1:4) Anything about us which is unclean, defiling, or degrading grieves Him.

He is the Spirit of wisdom and revelation. (Eph 1:17) Our ignorance, conceit, arrogance, or folly will grieve Him.

He is the Spirit of power, love and discipline. (2 Tim 1:7) If we are barren, fruitless, disorderly, confused, or out of control, it grieves Him.

He is the Spirit of Life. (Rom 8:2) Indifference, lukewarmness, dullness or deadness on our part grieves Him.

He is the Spirit of Glory. (I Peter 4:14) If we are worldly and overly concerned with the earth and the flesh, this grieves Him.

The Holy Spirit dwells within us to enable us "to grow up into Christ in all things." (Eph 4:13) He seeks to bring us daily into conformity to Christ's image (2 Cor 3:18) until we have reached "unto the measure of the statue of the fullness of Christ." (Eph 4:13) Anything that hinders this purpose grieves Him. If we knowingly or willfully permit anything contrary to what the Holy Spirit does to remain in us, this proves that we love sin more.

The second commandment to be considered here is "Quench not the Spirit." (I Thess 5:19) We grieve the Holy Spirit when we say "yes" to Satan. We grieve Him when we say "no" to God when He woos us into holiness and service.

It is the task of the Holy Spirit to get us to obey God's Word. Self-will is latent within unless we cast self out by the power of the Holy Spirit. The only cure for self-will is a deliberate choice to do the will of God in all things, all the time, at all cost.

All of the above emphases point up the importance of living a clean life. What are the means by which we are cleansed?

I John 1:7 tells us that we find cleansing in "the blood of Christ." For the sinner, the blood removes the guilt of sin. For the saint, the blood removes the pollution of sin.

What is the method by which we are cleansed? "If we confess our sins, He is faithful and just to forgive us our sins, and to cleanse us from all unrighteousness." (I John 1:9)

"And God, which knoweth the hearts, bear them witness, giving them the Holy Spirit, and put no difference between us and them, purifying their hearts by faith." (Acts 15:8, 9)

What is the measure of our cleansing? We are cleansed from all defilement of the flesh and spirit. (2 Cor 7:1) God demands a cleansing that reaches from our innermost desire to the outermost deed.

Some Christians have often wanted the fullness of the Spirit, but they harbor known sin, are willfully disobedient, and set up deliberate resistance to the will of God.

Study the experience Joshua had with the sin of Achan. (Josh 7:10-13) To overcome that sin, the people were required to put it aside, sanctify themselves, and then obey God. If Christians are to live clean lives, we must get rid of all sin and not grieve or quench the Holy Spirit; then we will carry out this divine imperative.

WHAT DOES IT MEAN TO BE PERFECT?
Matt 5:48

One of the most amazing verses in the Bible is Matt 5:48 where Jesus says, "Be ye therefore perfect, even as your Father which is in heaven is perfect." Not only is this amazing, but it is also a divine imperative. God commands us to be perfect! It is more amazing when Jesus said that our perfection approximates the perfection of God.

First, Jesus teaches that there is a certain kind of perfection required of man. "Be perfect." Look who is saying this. It is Jesus the Son of God Who says, "I am the truth." If we do not believe this, our unbelief makes Jesus a liar, but He is the truth. In a way, Jesus sums up all His teachings in this verse.

There are other Scriptural writers who provide us with passages to support this assertion of Jesus. Timothy writes to tell us that "All Scripture is given by inspiration of God—that the man of God may be perfect." (2 Tim 3:16,17)

Paul tells us that the purpose of all ministry is to bring about perfection. "He gave some apostles, and some prophets, and some evangelists, and some pastors and teachers; for the perfecting of the saints." (Eph 4:11-15)

Still further, Paul says perfection is the purpose of all teaching and preaching. "Christ in you, the hope of glory: whom we preach, warning every man, and teaching every man in all wisdom; that we may present every man perfect in Christ Jesus." (Col 1:27, 28)

Scripture teaches that God commands us to be perfect. In the Old Testament, we are told: "Thou shalt be perfect with the Lord thy God." (Deut 18:13) In the New Testament we are exhorted to obtain perfection: "Leaving the principles of the doctrine of Christ, let us go on to perfection." (Heb 6:1)

We see, also, in Scripture, that some men did obtain perfection: Noah was perfect in his generation—Gen 6:9; Abraham was admonished to "walk before me and be thou perfect." (Gen 17:1)

Some disciples obtained it. "Howbeit we speak wisdom among them that are perfect." (I Cor 2:6) Again, "Let us therefore, as many as be perfect, be thus minded." (Phil 3:15)

Second, the text also reveals the kind of perfection required. "Even as" your Father which is in heaven. The words "even as" show us that this is not the perfection of angels. It is not that of Adam. It is not like that of Christ, nor is it equal to maturity; rather, it is the perfection of God the Father. How is He perfect?

He is perfect in power, but that is beyond us.

He is perfect in knowledge, but that, too, is beyond us.

He is perfect in goodness and love. It is possible for us to reach this. One man, Barnabas, did. "He was a good man and full of the Holy Spirit." (Acts 11:24) So was Joseph. (Luke 23:50)

This perfection we are talking about is not of the head, but of the heart, goodness, love, and faith. But how can we know how to be perfect even in these matters? God is a Spirit; we are but men. We read in John 1:18, "No man hath seen God at any time." That is quite true, but Jesus declared Him. "No man hath seen God at any time; the only begotten Son. He hath declared Him." (John 1:18) Jesus said, further, "He that hath seen me hath seen the Father." (John 14:9) Thus, Jesus manifested God in human life so that we all could see and understand. "The Word was made flesh and dwelt among us."

(John 1:14) Jesus was perfect of heart, goodness, and faith, all of which we can see. We are to follow His example. "As He is, so are we in this world." (I John 4:17)

What are some of the ways Jesus manifested the kind of

perfection that we can have? First, He was perfectly submitted to God. He said, "Not my will but thine be done." So can it be with us. There must be no resistance, complaining, or fighting back.

Like Jesus, we may perfectly trust God. He did this at all times under all circumstances. We, like Job, can do this. He lost his family and all of his possessions and said of God, "Though he slay me, yet will I trust him." (Job 13:15)

Jesus loved God with a perfect love. (Matt 5:43-48) Such love covers even our enemies, and Jesus said that results in perfection. We can love God with all our heart. Paul told the Colossian Church to manifest "mercies, kindness, humbleness, meekness, long-suffering, forbearance, forgiveness and above all these things put on charity, which is the bond of perfectness." (Col 3:12-14)

Next, Jesus showed that perfect love leads to perfect loyalty. Our love and loyalty toward God is possible, but we must not forget that, as men, we are subject to making mistakes and errors due to ignorance. But God overlooks the head when the heart is perfect in loyalty.

Jesus manifested perfect obedience; so can we. Our performance may err, but our spirit can be right. We need to follow Paul's advice to the Colossian Church and pray for perfection. (Col 4:12) We can perfectly submit our will to God.

God is looking for hearts that are perfect toward Him. He wants hearts that are in complete submission to Him—perfect in trust, love, loyalty, and obedience. John tells us that those who obey God's Word in him "verily is the love of God perfected." (I John 2:5)

What kind of heart do you have? Is it perfect or unclean? Is there any evidence of the presence of pride, anger, jealousy or evilness? God can give us a perfect heart life.

We must be willing to have our hearts changed. We must crucify the self-life and all sin, consecrate ourselves fully to Him and trust Him now to give us a perfect heart. "For the eyes of the Lord run to and fro throughout the whole earth, to show himself strong in the behalf of those whose heart is perfect toward him." (2 Chron 16:9)

DID YOU KNOW THAT SANCTIFICATION IS THE WILL OF GOD FOR ALL ?
I Thess 4:3,7

The term sanctification is synonymous with the word holiness. It means the cleansing of the human heart from the corruption of sin. It is referred to as "the rest of faith," crucifying the old man; perfection and heart purity.

The evidences of carnality in the life of believers are many. The carnal Christian can be characterized by several marks:

    He lives a life of inner conflict—Rom 7:22, 23; Gal 5:19.

    He lives a life of repeated defeat—Rom 7:15,19.

    He lives a life of protracted infancy—I Cor 3:1, 2; Heb 5:12-14.

    He lives a life of barren fruitlessness—John 15:2.

    He lives a life of worldliness—James 4; I John 2:15,16.

Other evidences of carnality can be seen in manifestations of inward war, passions such as pride, self-will, lust, or any disposition contrary to the mind which was in Christ.

Paul told the Thessalonians, who were already Christian, that sanctification is "the will of God." This makes it one of God's divine imperatives.

If sanctification is God's will, then it is the obligation and privilege of every Christian believer. This command is just as much a command as "Thou shalt not steal." The Holy Spirit sheds light on the soul as to its inward depravity and applies this to the conscience of the believer. The believer ought to be clean.

If God commands it, and it is, therefore, an obligation, it is reasonable to believe that each true Christian may ask for this blessing with full assurance of getting it. One must be sure he is a child of God, then claim sanctification. Such a cleansing is based on self-surrender and complete consecration to God and willingness for the whole will of God to work in life.

How do we know this? To the Thessalonian people, Paul said, "For God has not called us unto uncleanness but unto holiness." (I Thess 4:7)

If this is God's will and holy purpose, how is this done? It is wrought by the Holy Spirit by a cleansing of the tendency to sin.

There are four types of sanctificatiion: (1) provisional sanctification was provided by Jesus; (Heb 13:12) (2)initial sanctification takes place at conversion when we are saved; (I Cor 6:11) (Heb 3:1) (3) preparatory sanctification is seen when Joshua exhorted the Israelites to sanctify themselves in crossing the Jordan River; (4) entire sanctification is for Christians. (I Thess 5:22, 23) Preparatory sanctification is a prerequisite for entire sanctification.

How shall this come about? First, believe it is God's will—Acts 2:38, 39. Here, all are promised the gift of the Holy Spirit. We must believe this because God said it; He promised it to us, for us, and in us.

Second, we must be willing that God's will should be done in us for our sanctification and holiness. Seeking sanctification is evidence that we want to do His will. The matter is between God and us. It takes a great resolution. Are we willing to be made willing? A true child of God is willing, so we should be willing to forsake every sin that we know. God never removes sin until we are willing for Him to do so. We should be willing to give all our good things to God. This means, if necessary, our friends, ambition, loved ones, money, time, talents, all we know and will know, and all we have or may have. We must be willing to say, "Lord, God, it is mine no longer, it is thine."

One may think that this standard is too high; however, sacrifice is necessary, but it results in God's approval.

Next, it takes faith. Paul told the Galatian Church, "We receive the promise of the Spirit through faith." (Gal 3:14) If we meet the condition of full surrender and consecration that is complete, then we can say, "Yes, Lord, I receive the fullness of your Spirit now." Then believe that you do, and the work is done.

After this, we are to trust God day by day to lead and keep us clean. We must believe in spite of feeling. Feeling will sooner or later break in upon us, so rejoice! To some people, great joy does come; to others, there is great assurance.

Be persistent in your belief. Don't give up when you are tempted to doubt. Look back and say there it was done.

Thus, sanctification is God's will for us, but we must "will" to be sanctified. Since God's heart is set on our holiness, He has provided an uttermost salvation for us "now."

Let us humble ourselves before God. Never mind the questions that arise, but believe God's promises, God's gift, and God's power to do it. Wait upon God; tarry and believe with desperate faith. Look to God, and He will fill you with His love.

WHAT DOES IT MEAN TO BE FILLED WITH THE HOLY SPIRIT?
Eph 5:18

Christians are admonished by command to be filled with the Holy Spirit.

Again, a command from God demands another divine imperative Christians may be filled with the Holy Spirit. What God commands, He will do. He also promises this. Jesus said, "If ye then, being evil, know how to give good gifts unto your children, how much more shall your Father give the Holy Spirit to them that ask Him." (Luke 11:13)

The Holy Spirit dwells in believers. (John 14:17; Rom 8:9) As the temple of God, the Holy Spirit lives within us, otherwise we would not be Christian. "No man can call Jesus Lord without the Holy Spirit." Thus, Christians may have the Spirit, but the question we deal with here is—does the Holy Spirit have us? It is one thing to be born of the Spirit; it is another thing to be filled with the Spirit.

What kind of life is the Spirit-filled life? First, it is a life of inner peace and unity. (John 14:29) There is no inner conflict. There can be peace, even when there is conflict without. There is no known practice of willful sin. Communion with God is not marred by a bad conscience..

Second, it is a life of habitual victory, not constant defeat. (I Cor 15:57) Not victories, but "the" victory, victory over sin and self. "We are more than conquerors." (Rom 8:37)

Third, it is a life of real inward victory, not mere outward victory. (2 Cor 7:1)

Fourth, it is a life of constant growth into Christlikeness. (2 Cor 3:18) We grow in greater knowledge and grace. It is a progressive growing—from glory to glory. It is growth in the fruit of the Spirit. (Gal 5:22)

Fifth, it is a life of devoted separateness. (John 17:16) The world has no place in us. It is a life of spiritual isolation and spiritual insulation.

Sixth, it is a life of supernatural power. (John 14:12) Its secret is stated in Acts 1:8: "Ye shall receive power."

Seventh, it is a life of winsome holiness. (I Peter 1:15, 16) We are called to be holy. It is not a sinless perfection, nor a faultless one, but it is blameless. (I Thess 5:2; Jude 24)

A heart of pure love is an attractive one. How does one become filled with the Spirit? There must be a complete separation from all known sin, an act of the will. There must be total consecration of the total person and a complete surrender to God of all we are and have. (Rom 12:1, 2)

Then we appropriate this provision by faith. If we ask for the Holy Spirit, He will be given. (Luke 11:13) After this, we must believe that God will purify our hearts by faith. (Acts 15:8, 9) Then we tarry until we are endued. (Acts 1:8)

WHAT HAVE YOU GIVEN TO GOD?
Mal 3:10

Among those who know God, one of the most amazing things is to realize how good God is to us. Out of His goodness comes provision for our salvation and meeting all our other needs. In fact, the Scriptures tell us that "the very goodness of God leads us to repentance." Even "while we were yet sinners, Christ died for us." (Rom 5:8) Yet men still despise and overlook His goodness. Their ungratefulness is tantamount to robbing God. It is imperative that we give.

Really, what do we have that is ours? Money? "The silver is mine and the gold is mine, said the Lord." (Haggai 2:8) Lands? "The land is mine, for ye are strangers and sojourners with me." (Lev 25:23) Possessions? "Whatsoever is under the whole heaven is mine." (Job 41:11) Did we earn wealth? "It is He that giveth power to get wealth." (Deut 8:19) Our lives? Not even them. "All souls are mine." (Ezek 18:4) We owe all to God—all that we are, have, expect to have and be.

From the very beginning, men have recognized an obligation to God. In the Old Testament we have the account of Cain and Abel bringing offerings to God. Abraham, Jacob and others brought tithes to God. This called for offering a tenth of possessions to Him.

But, today, men demand a non-interfering God; they want

self-government, self-possessions, self-arrangements, all of which leave no place for God.

The Apostle Paul instructed the church at Corinth about giving. "Now concerning the collection for the saints, as I have given order to the churches of Galatia, evenso do ye. Upon the first day of the week let every one of you lay by him instore, as God hath prospered him." (I Cor 16:1, 2) Such giving shall not be mechanical, nor grudgingly, but eagerly, as the Lord prospered us.

So, giving is a definite part of our worship. "God loveth a cheerful giver." (2 Cor 9:7)

Many years ago, Dr. A.T Pearson suggested seven ways of giving:

> The careless way—to every cause regardless of merit
> The inclusive way—as much as our love and responsibilities allow
> The lazy way—by raising money on the side for the church
> The self-denying way—by doing without things we need or want
> The systematic way—giving a steady, certain amount regularly
> The equal way—as much as others give
> The heroic way—we limit ourselves and give as much as we can to others. This was John Wesley's way: make all you can; save all you can; give all you can.

The Lord still watches the treasury. It is not what we put in but what we have left that counts. We can observe how some people give:

> From pity—they think God and His people need charity.
> From pride—some give extra, to be commended for it.
> From partiality—only because we like to
> From pressure—give drudgingly, not really giving to God.

Out of penury—Jesus illustrated this with an observation of the poor widow who gave her all.

The rule about giving follows: "Upon the first day of the week let every one of you lay by him in store as God hath prospered him." (I Cor 16:2)

Giving is a divine imperative because God requires it. Our failure to give causes us to rob God. (Mal 3:10) If people robbed God, living under the Law, what about us who live under grace? Grace is greater than the Law. This means that we can go beyond the tithe to show our love for God.God has gone out of His way to give to us. He gave His Son Jesus for our salvation. What will we give Him?

Tithing was given at the command of God. From Scripture we learn three essential things about tithing. First, God owns the tithe. (Lev 27:30) Second, the tithe is "holy unto the Lord." (Lev 27:22) It bears His name and nature. Third, the tithe is to be brought into the storehouse. (Mal 3:1-12)

Why was the Law of the tithe enacted? To preserve the worship of God and the ministry and to restrict the unrestrained use of property. We pay tithes; we do not give them.

What are the results of tithing? It affects the tither himself. Spiritually, it helps him to relate better to God. It also provides for God's house (Mal 3:10) and satisfies our obligation to give.

Tithing excites and motivates our gratitude to God for His goodness to us. It carries God into all phases of life—the home, the workplace, and elsewhere. It is a preventive to worldliness.

Tithing will help build the Kingdom of God. It will assist in spreading the Gospel throughout the world. It will mean the success of our churches. The church is often poor because of a lack of financial support. Men spend too much on self. Nine-tenths with God's blessing is far better than ten-tenths without it.

God has given all for us. What have we given for Him?

DO YOU KNOW GOD'S PLAN FOR YOUR LIFE?
Rom 12:1, 2

God has a plan for each individual in this life and in the life to come. It is imperative that each of us discovers that plan. God's plan for our lives is factual. When that plan is found and followed, happiness and success will follow.

The world knows nothing about God and the God-planned life. Even many Christians have failed to see it, even as it is revealed in the Bible. God created us; therefore, He knows us. He has a plan exactly suited to our needs. We can discover it; God has made provision for it.

God's plan is not only factual, but it is also reasonable. Generally, we have models to guide, blueprints for building and roadmaps for traveling.

As we study the universe, we see marvelous design and planning by God in His handiwork all around us. Man stands as the highest proof of God's creation, and He will not leave us in confusion.

God's plan is practical. Men have found this plan. Abraham left home for an unknown land because he believed in God's plan for his life. Other great Bible characters like Moses, David, and Joseph also found God's plan for their lives.

Christian literature is full of people who have found God's plan. Great Christians like John Wesley and David Livingstone are good examples as is Gladstone, the great politician. In fact, in all walks of life can be found those who have followed God's plan for their lives—doctors, lawyers, housewives and many others.

God's plan is Scriptural. David records for us in Psalm 139 the fact that God knows all about us—our thoughts, words, deeds, our past, present and future. Even the very hairs of our heads are numbered. God is aware of our tears and all of our needs. Thus, with this knowledge, God has a personal plan for us. The psalmist said of God, "I will instruct thee and teach thee in the way which thou shalt go." (Psa 32:8) This plan specifically is for God's children. Our text says, "I beseech you therefore, brethren, by the mercies of God, that ye present your bodies a living sacrifice, holy, acceptable unto God, which is your reasonable service." (Rom 12:1, 2) Because our plan comes from God, it is wonderfully detailed. It is a plan sure to be profitable to us, now as well as in the world to come.

The plan is also essential since we cannot plan our own lives. Sin often interferes in this matter. Only God knows the future. The will of God brings life-long blessings both now and in the future. God wants us to know His will. This is true, not only for ministers, but also for laymen. God needs Christian mothers, fathers, merchants, doctors, etc. In fact, God really commands us to obey His will and thus find His plan for our lives.

God's plan is knowable. Romans 12:1 speaks to the brethren. To become a brother in Christ, one must experience salvation and sanctification.

There must be an honest willingness to do God's will. Obedience is the secret to becoming a child of God and to discovering His plan for our lives. Not only do we find guidance by obeying the will of God, but also by watching circumstances around us.

One can use the consecrated advice of friends to help us find God's plan. Most certainly, prayer is necessary. If we are genuinely Christian, God will enable us to follow our best judgment and the guidance of the Holy Spirit to determine His will and life-plan for us. It is imperative, therefore, that we come to know God's plan for our lives.

DO YOU KNOW GOD'S PLAN OF THE AGES?

The Grand Subjects of Prophecy

The Nations. One needs to study carefully what the Bible teaches about the nations. The Prophet Daniel is a major source for this study. There is much happening among the nations of earth now. Some are even afraid that there are enough destructive forces to destroy the world, but God will step in and control this situation since He has a plan for the earth and the nations that occupy it.

The Jews. Someone has estimated that there are over two million Jews in Palestine. Israel is now an independent state for the first time since Nebuchadnezzar 2000 years ago. A dead language has come alive, so some prophecy has been fulfilled. This brings all prophecy into focus. God has a plan for His people.

The Church. The church is changing, probably more than in the past Reformation. Many of the signs predicted by Jesus are now evident. God has a plan for the Church, and the Book of Revelation reveals that plan.

The Heavens and the Earth. The heavens and the earth are constantly in today's news. Prophecy reveals a great deal in store for both. Much emphasis is being placed on space exploration, but man cannot hide from God in the midst of the stars. (Obad 4; Amos 9:2) God has a plan for the heavens and the earth; His redemptive plans will not be thwarted for things physical as well as things spiritual.

The Importance of Plans

<u>Men Have Planned</u>. A study of history reveals many efforts by men to plan for the conquest of the world. In the past, great nations of Assyria, Babylon, Medo-Persia and Rome made such plans. Great generals like Alexander the Great of Greece conquered the then known world and later wept that there were no more worlds to conquer. In the recent past, Germany, under Hitler, sought to dominate the world. Communism in Russia had the same goal; however, all of these, and others have failed.

<u>God Has a Plan</u>. This plan, we are told by Paul in the Ephesian letter, was formulated before the foundation of the world. (Eph 3:11) His plan is far-reaching from eternity past to eternity future and involves, we believe, the entire universe. There is no end and no limit to the Kingdom of God.

His plan is really beyond our fullest understanding, yet God has revealed it to us. It is the only plan that will succeed and last forever. The Bible is the revelation of God's purposes and plans for mankind and the earth. There is design all around us for study.

The reader is referred to Chart Number One, the writer's prophetic chart entitled "God's Plan of the Ages." It is recommended that one should start on the left hand side of the chart and follow development as we go along in our studies.

The Concept of Ages

<u>Importance of Ages</u>. It is helpful in understanding the Bible to recognize that there are divisions in its contents. A correct knowledge of these divisions will give one a key to understanding what the Bible teaches.

Chart 1

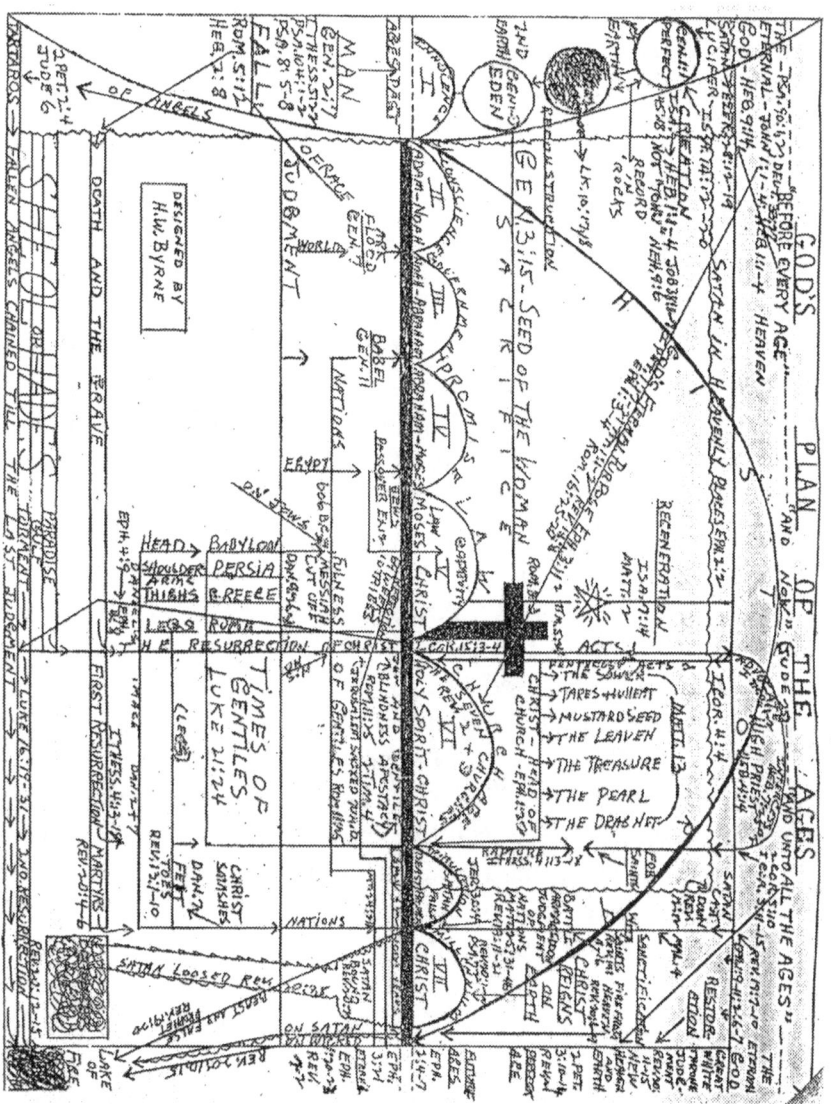

The divisions of Scripture are referred to as "ages." The Greek word for ages is AION, (pronounced I-on). There are several places in the English New Testament where this word is translated "world" when the Greek word is really "ages." The New Testament was first written in Greek and then translated into English. The term age is used in Eph 2:7 and Col 1:26.

The following Scripture in the King James Version uses "world," but the word "age" is better. Matt 39:40-49 is an example. Matt 24:3, "What shall be the sign of thy coming and of the end of the age?" Other illustrations include Lk 1:70; I Cor 10:11; Heb 1:2; 9:26. These passages show a succession of ages in the history of the earth and world.

These ages were "planned by God." (Heb 1:2) He ordained the ages through Jesus Christ. In spite of Satan and sin, God planned these ages as a part of the overall Plan of the Ages. One can refer to Chart No. One to identify them. They vary in length and purpose.

There are other Scriptural terms which show that there are Biblical ages. The word "forever" is often used in the Old Testament, written in the Hebrew language. Two words should be noted. One is the word OLAM, (pronounced "oh-lam"), which means literally "to hide or conceal." This word refers to "the eternity of the past." As used in Prov 8:22, 23, it can be translated "before the creation of the world." It is also used in Gen 21:33; Isa 40:28; Deut 33:37; Psa 93:2 to speak of "the everlasting God Who existed 'before' creation." OLAM also refers to the eternity of the past as "age to age." See Psa 90:2 on Chart No. One. "From everlasting to everlasting, thou art God." Here is proof that there were "ages before the creation of the world." Other places show OLAM to mean eternity of the future and its ages.

The second word is AD, translated "forever," and it also means in the Hebrew "to press on," "forward," and "advance." Isa 57:15 speaks of God Who "inhabits eternity."

AD here means that God is marching on, progressing through eternity.

We can draw certain conclusions from our study of OLAM and AD:

    1. Eternity—past, present and future—is divided

into ages.
2. This eternity progresses and moves onward into unlimited ages to come.

There are two words in New Testament usage, written first in the Greek language, which refer to the concept of "forever": AIDOS, (pronounced I-de-os), and AION, (pronounced I-on).

AION in some places refers to the "present" age. Matt 13:22; Mk 11:14; Heb 1:2; 11:3; Lk 16:8; 20:4; Rom 12:12; 2 Cor 4:4; Gal 1:4. It also refers to the Christian dispensation as used in Matt 13:39; 24:3; 28:19, 20, and others. It refers to the Millennial Era in Matt 12:31, 32; Lk 20:34-36; and others. It means further "all eternity of the Future." Rom 1:25; 9:5; 11:36. Still further it also means "throughout all eternity." Matt 21:19; John 8:51; Luke 1:51 and others. Again, it means "into the ages of ages." This shows that the future is divided into ages. This is found in Rom 16:27; Gal 1:5; Phil 4:20; I Tim 1:17; 2 Tim 4:18; Heb 13:21. In the Book of Revelation, it is noted in 1:6; 4:9,10; 5:13; 10:6; 11:15; 15:7 and 22:5.

In the Book of Jude we find a summary of this matter:

1. Before every age—means "before the creation."
2. And now—a period called "time or history."
3. And unto all the ages—future eternal ages.

Consult Chart No. One at the extreme left to see the eternity of the Past; the extreme right, the eternity of the future; and the middle, time or the present.

<u>Ages of the Past</u>. Thus, we see that the Bible speaks particularly of ages. There are ages past, the present age, and ages to come. In his letter to the Ephesians in Chapter Three, Verse 11, Paul refers to the manifold wisdom of God expressed through His "eternal purpose in Christ Jesus our Lord." The marginal reading refers to God's purposes of the ages. We deal now with ages past.

Ages past focuses our attention on the eternity of the past. The Psalmist said, "Before the mountains were brought forth, or ever thou hadst formed the earth and the world, even from everlasting to everlasting thou art God." (Psa 90:2) This could also read "from age to age" thou art God.

Gen 1:1 says, "In the beginning God." In Rev. 1:8, John speaks of God as the Alpha and Omega, the beginning and the ending. From these verses, and others which could be cited, we learn that God had no beginning and will have no ending. He has existed from eternity and will exist through eternity.

There was a time when God alone existed as Spirit. He chose to come out of His unknown existence in the past and create the heavens and the earth. In time He brought man into existence. Scriptures imply that there were other intelligent beings, known as angels, which were brought also into existence. As to when this was done, we have no information.

The Present Ages. These ages began immediately following the creation by God and will continue until Jesus returns, sets up His Kingdom, and leads us into new ages to come.

Bible scholars have divided the present ages into at least three dispensations—the Father, the Son, and the Holy Spirit. Each of these dispensations can be divided further into subdivisions as follows:

1. The Age of Innocence—the age of Adam and Eve
2. The Age of Conscience—the age from Adam to Noah
3. The Age of Government—the age from Noah to Abraham
4. The Age of Promise—the age from Abraham to Moses
5. The Age of Law—the age from Moses to Christ
6. The Age of the Church—the age of Christ and the Holy Spirit
7. The Age of Christ—the Age of His Kingdom

There appear to be six phases to God's plan:

1. Creation
2. Reconstruction
3 Regeneration
4. Revelation

5. Sanctification
6. Restoration

The segment of time stretching from the creation of Adam and Eve to the end of the Age of the Millennium we call history. Involved are history (time past) and prophecy (history written in advance).

The Ages to Come. Eternity Ahead. These ages will include the future world of Christ and the Church in the building of the Kingdom of God on earth, the redemption of the earth during the Millennium, the new heavens and new earth, the perfect age (2 Peter 3:10-14), and many future ages spoken of by Paul (Eph 2:4-7; 3:21; Rev 22)

The Creation of the Universe

The Creator. God was the Creator. The "Word" of God was His method. "The worlds were formed by the Word of God Who was the Son of God." (Heb 11:3) As Pre-existent God, He was the divine instrument by which this was done. (John 1:1-4)

"In the beginning GOD." (Gen 1:1) In the eternity of the past, the eternal God once existed alone.

1. He was the Eternal Father—Deut 33:27; Psa 90:2; Rev 1:8; Isa 57:15.

2. He was the Eternal Son—co-equal and co-eternal with the Father—John 1:1, 2, 14; Heb 1:1-4.

3. He was the Eternal Spirit—co-equal with the Father and the Son—Heb 9:14.

4. He was the Eternal Triune God—3 in 1; yet one God.

The literal translation of Gen 1:1, "In the beginning Gods (plural) created the heavens and the earth." A plural noun but a singular verb.

5. He was a Trinity in unity—Deut 6:4.

Thus, we can define God as an eternal personal being of absolute knowledge, power and goodness (holiness). This eternal God has an eternal purpose which includes creation and redemption through Jesus Christ. (Eph 1:3-11; 3:11)

The Creative Act. "In the beginning God created the heavens and the earth." (Gen 1:1) What was involved in that creation? "Thou, even thou, art Lord alone; thou hast made heaven, the heaven of heavens, with all their host; the earth, and all things that are therein; and thou preservist them all; and the host of heaven worshippeth thee." (Neh 9:6) This was the first phase of God's plan.

The Method. Nothing is revealed in the above passage as to how the creation was done. The word "created" means creation out of nothing; not made. The Hebrew word for create is BARA, to form something out of nothing.

Herbert Spencer, the skeptic, tried to discount the creative act by saying that creation required five factors: (1) time, (2) space, (3) matter, (4) force, and (5) motion. It is to be noted that all five of these factors are found in Gen 1:1. As previously mentioned, the Word of God was the method. Jesus Christ, the Son, was the instrument.

The Nature of Heaven. The Scriptures give us some idea of what the created heaven was like:
1. Everlasting—Psa 80:29
2. Immeasurable—Jer 31:37
3. High—Psa 103:11
4. Holy—Psa 20:6; Isa 57:15
5. God's dwelling place—I Kings 8:30; Matt 6:9
6. God's throne—Isa 66:1; Acts 7:49
7. Angels present—created by God—Mk 9:6; Col 1:16— "For by Him were all things created whether in heaven or in earth."

In Isa 14:13, mention is made of the "sides of the north." Here it is implied that this is a mysterious statement about the place of heaven.

The Character of the Created Earth. Note Isa 45:18: "Thus saith the Lord that created the heavens; God Himself that formed the earth and made it; He hath established it, He created it; 'not in vain.' 'He formed it to be inhabited' ; I am the Lord and there is none else." Note the following:
1. God created the earth.

2. God created the earth for a purpose (not in vain).
3. God created the earth to be inhabited.
4. God created the earth out of nothing. The word BARA is translated this way.

Job 38:1-7 reveals that the angels sang after God got through creating the earth. Later on when the earth was reconstructed, the word ASAH was used, which means made not created.

<u>The Purpose of God's Creation</u>. Isa 45:15 says, "He formed it to be inhabited." This original earth was created pure and holy with no trace of sin or rebellion. God desired to use the earth as the proving ground for intelligent creatures of choice before He moved them to heaven with Himself. All of the laws of earth acted in harmony with each other, and there was nothing created "in vain" or "without form," as translated in Gen 1:2.

From this account we have no hint that there were any creatures of choice existing in God's universe previous to the creation of earth; consequently, there was no sin at that time.

<u>Earth's First Inhabitants</u>. We commonly think of man as the first creature of choice and reason; however, that is a mistake. As we have seen, God brought into existence angels who sang when He created the earth, the hosts of heaven. They populated heaven when He created it.

The Scriptures reveal that one of these angels governed the earth. Job 1:6, 7 states, "Now there was a day when the sons of God (angels) came to present themselves before God, and Satan came also among them. And the Lord said unto Satan, whence commeth thou? Then Satan answered the Lord and said, from going to and fro in the earth and walking up and down in it."

Here is one called Satan who inhabited the earth. Who is he? Apparently he was a viceroy of God who lived in the original Eden. Apparently, also, when the angels appeared before God they reported their work. Perhaps here we get a picture of the probation of angels.

> Ezek 28:14, 15, 17
> Thou art the anointed cherub that covereth; and I

have set thee so; thou wast upon the holy mountain of God, thou hast walked up and down in the midst of the stones of fire. Thou wast perfect in thy ways from the day thou wast created, till iniquity was found in thee. Thine heart was lifted up because of thy beauty; thou hast corrupted thy wisdom by reason of thy brightness; I will cast thee to the ground.

Isa 14:12, 13
How thou art fallen from heaven, O Lucifer, son of the morning How art thou cast down to the ground, which did weaken the nations. For thou hast said in thine heart, I will ascend into heaven, I will exalt my throne above the stars of God; I will sit also upon the mount of the congregation, in the sides of the north; I will ascend above the heights of clouds; I will be like the Most High. Yet thou shalt be brought down to hell.

What do we learn from these passages? It is apparent that some of the angels failed their probation. Peter says, "God spared not the angels that sinned (with Satan) but cast them down to hell, and delivered them into chains of darkness to be reserved unto judgment." (2 Peter 2:4)

Jude 6
The angels which kept not their first estate, but left their own habitation (heaven), He hath reserved in everlasting chains under darkness into the judgment of the great day.

Here is described an angel called Lucifer or Satan who had access to the newly created earth but who rebelled against God and tried to usurp God's throne. The reason— pride entered his heart, and this led to sin, and sin led to rebellion. The result—Lucifer and one-third of the angels in heaven that he influenced were cast out of heaven into the earth. This is strengthened by Jesus' words:

Divine Imperatives

Luke 10:17,18
And the seventy returned with joy, saying, Lord even the devils are subject unto us through thy name. And He said to them, I beheld Satan as lightning fall from heaven.

The result—when cast out, Satan and his group of angels in rebellion destroyed the beauty of the earth that God had created and over which Satan ruled. Satan remained here as the Prince of the Power of the Air. (Eph 2:2)

Chart 2

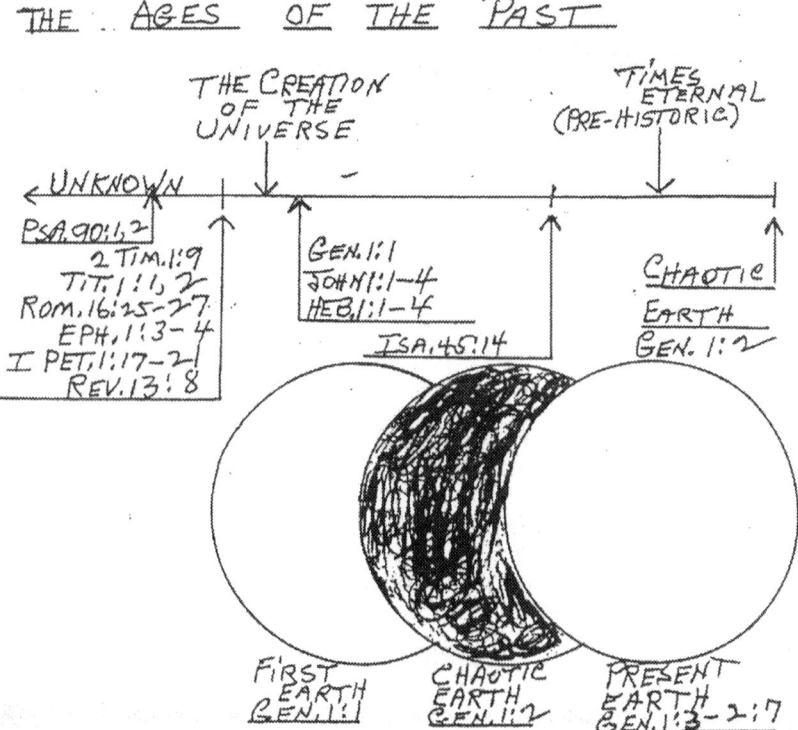

Chart Number Two shows what happened.

Pre-historic Times

<u>The Period of Times Eternal.</u>In Gen 1:1 we saw that God created a universe that was perfect. As we move to Gen 1:2, we see chaos (see Chart No. 2 above). Here we are told that the earth "was" without form. This was not true in Verse one—the beginning. The verb "was without form" may also be translated "became." It is the Hebrew word TOHU, meaning "became without form." The word is so used in Gen 19:26 where we read that Lot's wife became (TOHU), a pillar of salt. Thus, a perfectly created earth, originally, became without form and void. This apparently was what Jeremiah saw (Jer 4:23-27) when he, too, saw a time when the earth was "without form and void; and the heavens, they had no light."

The term "times eternal" is used in Rom 16:25 to refer to "since the world began" or since "times eternal." Grace was kept secret since "times eternal." We read in 2 Tim 1:9 that grace was provided in Christ before "times eternal." In Titus 1:2 eternal life was said to be promised before "times eternal."

We can conclude, therefore, that a time gap existed from the time of creation in Verse One to the time when chaos took place.

How long was this period? No one knows, but it began "right after" God created the universe. The record is in the rocks. The Scriptures speak of this period as "times eternal." We can draw certain conclusions:

1. God created in the beginning.
2. Then began the period known as "times eternal," or prehistoric times.
3. During this period the earth was perfect and beautiful.
4. Prehistoric animals could have roamed the fields and streams of this original earth.
5. After this unknown period of time, earth "became" chaotic. (Gen 1:2)

If one accepts this "gap" theory, this will allow for prehistoric animals and plants and will harmonize with primitive science which says the earth is millions of years old. In fact, some scientists now place the age of the earth between four and nine million years.

There is also a speculative theory that man-like creatures existed at that time. Some speculate further that the remains of such creatures have been discovered by archaeologists. If such is the case, these creatures appeared before the creation account of man in Genesis. Thus, they were not created, as man was, in the image of God.

The Wrecking of the Original Earth. In Genesis 1:7 we see that the original earth "became chaotic." It was in ruins. God did not originally create it this way as recorded in Genesis 1:1. Now, the earth has all the marks of a number of catastrophes like this, perhaps with billions of years of normal conditions in between. This is perhaps how the oil, coal, and other natural resources so necessary for modern times were formed.

What was the cause of this wreckage? There is very little in the Bible to answer this question. Suspicion, however, falls on Satan. Evidently there was a rebellion led by Satan and his angels, Satan lived before the creation of earth (Ezek 28:14, 15, 17) already referred to. Evidently he had charge or governorship over the original earth. Apparently he was a viceroy of God. Job 1 describes his report to God.

Something happened to cause Satan to rebel against God. As we have previously seen, Isa 14:12 as well as Ezek 28 imply that Satan was an archangel who lived in a crystal palace of precious stones. He was the "anointed cherub." Then he fell from God's favor, influencing some of the angels to follow him in rebellion against God. Evidently he wanted to become God and was proud of his appearance and place of honor. The result was he and the fallen angels were cast out of heaven. Sin originated here. When Satan said, " I will," as opposed to God's will, sin was born.

The result? Possessing enormous power, Satan and his fallen group destroyed the original earth. The following conditions prevailed on this chaotic earth:
> The earth became submerged in water.
> This could have been caused by a large star,
> controlled by Satan, coming too close to the earth.
> Darkness enveloped the earth—Jer 4:23-29; 38:1-11.
> Satan was left to roam the earth as the prince of the
> power of the air. Eph 2:2

> The angels, which fell with Satan, were placed in chains in a special hell called tartaros. Jude 6; 2 Peter 2:4

Why was Satan allowed to remain? First, perhaps he had a legitimate claim on owning the fallen earth. You will recall that he offered Jesus rulership of the earth if He would obey Satan; Jesus, apparently, did not dispute Satan's claim.

Second, God has chosen not to rule the universe by sheer force. He rules, rather, according to His nature. He chose to respect the rights of free moral agents.

Third, God gave Satan his <u>permitted</u> appointment to rule the original earth, but Satan rebelled. God plans to dispossess Satan and banish him, but He will do it in such a way that even Satan will have to admit that God has been true, recognizing the rights of all.

God is now putting down rebellion, but He is doing it according to the law of holiness rather than that of force. This is why the cross is necessary. It is also why Jesus "will return" to finish the work.

God appointed Satan, and he will hold his place until a worthy successor can be found and qualified. God placed man here to test him with the hope that he would rule the earth, but man failed.

Thank God a Successor has been found, even Jesus, Son of Man, Son of God, and the Second Adam. Presently, Satan is a "provincial" governor of earth, and he rules by permission. God is the Supreme Ruler of the whole universe, and His will is supreme.

<u>The Reconstruction of the Earth.</u> We now reach the second phase of God's plan—reconstruction or renovation. God set about to restore the earth to its original condition.

How was this done? In Gen 1:2 we read (following chaos), "And the Spirit of God moved upon the face of the waters." In Deut 32:11, the word "move" is translated "flutter." Here is a sacred and beautiful picture of the Holy Spirit, the third Person of the Trinity, fluttering over the earth.

There are some pertinent observations to make at this point:

1. It was the Son of God Who created the universe and original earth as recorded in Gen 1:1. See also Heb 1:1, 2.

2. The reconstruction of the earth was done by the Holy Spirit.

Gen 1:2b. This shows that the Holy Spirit did not create. His business is to re-create, to take the work of the Son and re-create or restore it. He does this also in the regeneration of a lost soul.

3. The work of the Holy Spirit took six days to reconstruct the earth, to repair it. Thus, the Bible does not teach that the earth was created in six days.

Refer to Chart No. Three below.

Chart 3

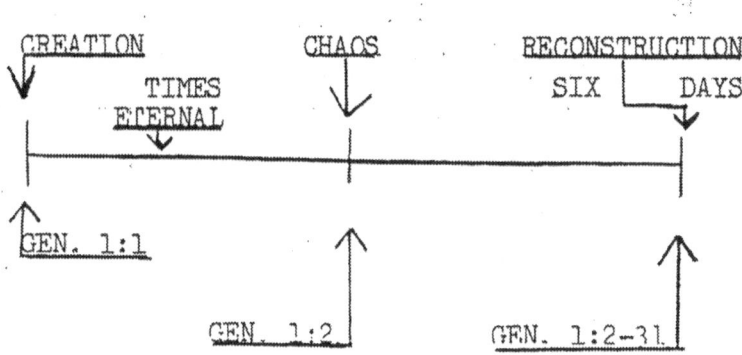

4. The theories of interpretation regarding the six days of reconstruction have emerged. One view takes the position that the six days refer to "long periods of time," or long days. Another view claims that the Holy Spirit took six days to accomplish this.

The "process" of reconstruction by the Holy Spirit involved one of separation. Following is a listing of the work of the six days:

1. Day One—separation of light from darkness

This was not the creation of light because the sun was not replaced until the fourth day. It must have been either cosmic light or the presence of God Who is Light, probably the latter.

2. Day Two—separation of the waters

Water was over all the earth; some water was removed from the surface and put above the earth. The sub-zero temperature up there probably froze the water and formed the ice envelope. This created a uniform climate as heat was radiated equally to all parts of the earth. There is evidence for this. Tropical grass has been found at the north pole where tropical animals were found frozen with it in their mouths. Quite likely this ice envelope was broken up in Noah's flood; the animals were caught, and the ice age began.

Around 1950 some scientists, according to a report in the New York Times, discovered evidence of a water canopy around the earth. Later on, astronauts reported the same thing.

There was only one continent then—Gen 1:9. Later the earth was split into continents. See Gen 10:25 for Biblical proof of this.

A recent article in Time magazine (May 27, 1996) describes the recent findings of paleontologists which indicate that at one time the earth consisted of one big land mass. Therefore, great dinosaurs were able to exist all over the world. These reports were published in the journal Science and in National Geographic. Further evidence points to a time when the earth split into separate continents.

3. Day Three
Water was separated from the land, and plant life appeared.

4. Day Four
Night was separated from day; the sun, moon, and stars appeared.

5. Day Five
Living creatures appeared in the air and sea.

6. Day Six
Living creatures appeared on land, and man was created.

7. Day Seven
The Sabbath was established; God rested. He moved from work to rest.

God, the Holy Spirit, finished the work of reconstruction and pronounced everything good. (Gen 1:31)

The Creation of Man

<u>Original Man.</u> In Gen 2:7 we read the following:

> "And God formed man of the dust of the ground and breathed into his nostrils the breadth of life; and man became a living soul."

From this verse we see that God "created" man, a three-fold creature who was responsible to his Creator. (I Thess 5:23) Note some observations of this creative act of God:

1. Man was "formed" from the dust of the earth; he was given a body.
2. God breathed life into man. This was God's life and made man a spiritual being.
3. Man became a soul. Soul-life consists of mind, feelings, and will. Man's soul-life makes each individual distinctive and different from others.
4. Man was capable of fellowship with one another and God. Beasts do not have this ability
5. Man's personality
    Man has spirit—God-consciousness.
    Man has soul—self-consciousness.
    Man has body—world-consciousness.
6. Originally, man was clothed with a garment of light.
    Psa 104:1, 2.
7. In the beginning, man and animals were vegetarians.
    Gen 1:29, 30
8. Man was given dominion over the earth. Gen 1:28—he was an earth ruler.
    This involved all creatures on earth, but this dominion was limited under God's authority.
9. Man's purpose was to be fruitful.
    He was to multiply, to "replenish" the earth.

10. He was to be earth's Second Governor.
   He was to be tested to prove his qualifications to rule.

The Ages of the Earth—Present Time

(See Chart No. One marked I through VII Ages)

<u>The Age of Innocence</u>. With this age we begin the study of Historic Time. The Scriptural record of this age is found in Gen 1:26, 27 to 3:24. Certain facts stand out in this age:

1. Length—from the time of man's creation to his expulsion from the Garden of Eden—the time unknown, but thought to be about 130 years

2. Purposes of this age:
    To see if man could succeed Satan as earth ruler—Psa 8:4-8; Gen 1:28
    To provide man a choice whereby he could become righteous
    To see if man would <u>voluntarily</u> obey—Gen 2:15-17
        God wanted voluntary obedience, holiness and righteousness; a test was required to secure it.
        Great glory is brought to God through <u>voluntary</u> obedience;
        machine-like obedience is not desirable.
        If man had been incapable of sinning, he would not have been a free moral agent and therefore could not give voluntary obedience.
    To choose the good, the <u>possibility</u> of evil was necessary; disobedience was the alternative, and it had the possibility of evil within it.

3. The events of this age:
    Man was created innocent, God-like, and a free, moral agent.

Gen 1:26, 27; 2:7; I Thess 5:23
He was placed in a perfect Eden. Gen 2: 8-15
Man's responsibility was to hold dominion over the earth and pass the test of probation.
Satan was allowed to test man. Gen 3
> He appeared to tempt Adam and Eve.
> Man failed the test since he sinned. Gen 3:6

4. Consequences of the Fall of Man—Gen 3:14-19; Rom 5:12, 18, 19

Man lost his God-likeness. Gen 3:7
Man lost his raiment of light.
> Nakedness is a reminder of that fact.
> It proclaims the need of the garment of salvation.
> Adam and Eve tried to regain Godlikeness through a covering of fig leaves, but man cannot clothe himself and make himself fit for God's presence.
> Man's nature became corrupt. Rom 5:5-8

Sin separated man from God. Gen 3-8
> It always does so.
> The only way back is through the cross.

Sin distorted man's vision of God Who loves him and seeks to save Him. Gen 3:9,10
> Why were Adam and Eve afraid? God had been a close friend; Sin brought fear.
> Man cannot and need not hide from God.

Satan maintained governorship of the earth. I Cor 4:4; Eph 2:2
> Man had disqualified himself to be earth governor. Heb 2:8

The earth was cursed—thorns and thistles, and destroying germs began to plague the physical earth; the animals became wild and carnivorous. Gen 3:17-19

Man was cursed with death. Gen 2:17; Rom 5:12
> The grave was made necessary.
> Hell (Hades and Sheol) was also made necessary.
> Man's spirit died; he lost his God-consciousness and became self-conscious and world-conscious. Prov

20:20; Eph 2:1

Man would probably have died physically in the Garden had not Jesus, the Lamb of God, been offered before the foundation of the world.

  The immediate result

    Great sin was practiced, and the judgment of God was pronounced on it.

    Adam and Eve were expelled from Eden. Gen 3:22-24

God could have blotted all out, but He chose the path of redemption

    For man

    Also for the physical earth

5. The first promise of a Redeemer - Gen 3:15

    The seed of the woman - not man

    The seed should "bruise" the Serpent's head.

    The "heel" of the seed to be bruised

      Prophetic of the Saviour's death

      Gen 3:21—clothes provided through the death of a substitute

    (Lk 15:22)

    God removed the fig leaves

    Evidently, Adam and Eve were saved by sacrifice, (Gen 2:21) although Adam's name is not mentioned among the great ones in Heb 11.

6. The end of the Age of innocence

    Seth became head of the theocratic line after Cain killed Abel.

    Seth was born when Adam was 130 years old.

    Expulsion from the Garden took place before this.

    Cain and Abel were born after the expulsion, also.

<u>The Age of Conscience</u>. Scriptural coverage of this age is Gen 4:1 to 8:22.

1. The length of this period - from Eden to the Flood - about

1526 years

2. Purposes of this age
    To test man under conscience; to see if man wanted his own way
    To show man he needs a Saviour, that he cannot save himself
        God has let man try every method, and He used this to show Him his need.
        Man is slow to learn because of his own sin and weakness.
    To show there was a semblance of a revelation during this age through Noah, the prophet
    To reveal that through disobedience man received the knowledge of good and evil
    To indicate that under conscience man was left to his choice between good and evil
    To give God a chance to test man by letting him go his own way

3. Events of this age
    The first child was born to Adam and Eve. Gen 4:1
        Eve thought Cain would fulfill the redemptive provision stated in Gen 3:15, but he didn't.
    Other children could have been born to them; Abel was not necessarily the second child.
    Cain and Abel were representative men: Cain of bad men and Abel of good men.
    God accepted Abel's offering, but rejected Cain's. Gen 4:3-7
        Abel's offering was "blood sacrifice," but Cain's was not. (Vs.3, 4)
        Heb 9:22 shows blood was required.
    Here was the beginning of false religion—that of works.
    Cain murdered his brother Abel. Gen 4:8
    It was a time of great culture and city-building. Gen 4:16-24
    The godly Enoch was born and was later translated. Gen 5:18, 21-24
    Eve bore Seth who started what was known as the godly line. Gen 4:25, 26
    Noah was born. Gen 5:28, 29

4. Results
   Left to his own way, man failed and great wickedness resulted. Gen 6:1-8
   - Self-will led to great sin.
   - All restraint was removed. Gen 6:5
   - The unregenerate heart does not change.

   Under conscience man failed the test.
   God postponed judgment for 120 years. Gen 6:3
   A great compromise took place. Gen 6:5, 6
   - Fallen angels, called sons of God, took bodies and cohabited with the daughters of men.
   - Why? To corrupt the godly line which would provide the Saviour.
   - This was a special kind of union that would have corrupted the human race.
   - It was an unnatural union that brought forth a new race called Nephilum, (also called giants).
   - Wicked spirits before and after the flood have had direct dealings with human beings.

   But God rejected all of this; "all flesh" became corrupt, and God planned destruction. Gen 6:3, 5-7,12

5. But Noah found grace in the Lord's eyes. Gen 6:8
   - Noah was a just man and perfect in his generation; he walked with God. Gen 6:9
   - He begat three sons: Shem, Ham, and Japheth.

6. The Flood
   - The Flood came as judgment on a sinful world.
   - God instructed Noah to prepare an Ark that he, his family, and therace might be perpetuated. Gen 6:14 - 8:19
   - Judgment came to this age at its end. Gen 7:11,13, 17-24

<u>The Age of Human Government.</u> The Scriptural coverage for this age is Gen 8:20; 11:9.

1. Length from the Flood to the Tower of Babel; from Noah to

Abraham about 430 years
> It began with Noah's altar and ended with the rebellion at Babel, and the call to Abraham.

2. Purposes of this age
> To test men under governmental law
> To show the inadequacy of human law to solve man's problems

3. Events of this age
> After the Flood
>> Noah built an altar unto the Lord. Gen 8:20, 21
>> An altar in the Old Testament speaks of sacrifice. Heb 11:7
>> Noah was saved because he believed the promise of Gen 3:15.
>> He looked ahead to the cross.
>> This is a revelation of the "scarlet thread" of salvation; God is merciful in the midst of judgment; salvation is only by the cross.
> Every dispensation begins at the place of sacrifice; ends with man's departure from it.

4. God's covenant with Noah - Gen 8:2 - 9:27
> God promised never to destroy the earth again by water; He gave a rainbow as a sign. Gen 8:21;9:9-17
> God promised never to interrupt the seasons again. Gen: 8:22
> Man was allowed to eat meat. Gen 9:3
>> But he could not eat blood. Gen 9:4
>> Blood was typical of the cross.
> God gave man governmental law. Gen 9:6
>> Before the Flood, every man did as he pleased; the result -sin, corruption and death.
>> This law was not a part of the law of Moses.
>> It has never been abrogated.
>> The purpose of government was to restrain sin.

It is a minister of God. Rom 13:4
Capital punishment was instituted.

5. Results
    Man failed to govern himself.
        Noah began well with the covenant. Gen 9:1
        Man failed; even Noah got drunk. Gen 9:21
        Man needs the control of Christ.
    The nations were formed. Gen 10:1-5, 20, 31, 32
    The original continent of the earth was split into present continents, probably to care for the geographical distribution of the nations. Gen 10:24, 25 This happened in the days of Peleg. Gen 10:25 Peleg means "division," probably named after the mighty division of the earth. We are not told how this division took place; it could have happened in the Flood.

6. Nimrod, the mighty hunter
    Nimrod was born. Gen 10:8-10
        He was a great hunter and leader.
        He organized a kingdom called Babel. (Vs.10)
        Nimrod means "rebel"; "before the Lord" means he defied God.
    Nimrod organized a rebellion. Gen 11:1-9
        Union and a world empire were planned. (Vs.4)
        He built a great city and tower to make a name for themselves, but God ordered them to scatter out and replenish the earth.
        God quelled the uprising. Gen 11:5-9
        God came down and confounded the languages (Gen ll:9) and scattered them over the earth.
    Archaeology reveals that there at Babel the mystery religions originated. Evidently Nimrod and his wife started these religions. Some think that his wife Semiramis was an evil priestess. She claimed to have given birth supernaturally to her son Tammiz and that he had no earthly father. Apparently Satan sought here to imitate the

Incarnation.
This false religion spread to other lands later on, emphasizing the mother-son combination.
> Isis and Horus in Egypt
> Aphrodite and Eros in Greece
> Venus and Cupid in Italy, and others

Other mysteries originated here such as holy wafers, holy water, etc.

7. Final results
    Man failed to govern himself.
    Judgment came from God. Gen 11:5-9

<u>The Age of Promise.</u> The Scriptural coverage for this age includes Gen 11:10; Exodus 19:2

1. Length - about 427 years (Gal 3:17) from the Promise to the Exodus, from Abraham to Mount Sinai

2. Purposes of this age
    To test men under a promise of grace
    To test the witness of a nation called Israel
    To prepare for the coming Messiah
    To show that environment, culture and eduation are not sufficient to save man

3. Events of this age
    Abraham was called. Gen 12:1
    Why did God call Abraham?
        To show sin, guilt, the ruin of the race and man's need of a Saviour
        To reveal that he was the best of men, had good environment and descendants, but man failed under these circumstances.
        To have Israel write the Bible - Rom 3:1, 2
        To be a channel for the Messiah - Gen 12:3; 26:4; 28:14

John 8:56; Gal 3:16
To be a witness to the heathen world, but there was failure all down the line

God's covenant with Abraham - Gen 12:1-3
- This covenant was made 430 years "before" Sinai.
- It concerns Israel and Israel's land primarily, but points also to the spiritual descendants of Abraham - the Church.
- This covenant shows what was in the heart of God, His Grace. Notice the I's, not Abraham's merit.
- God prospered Abraham. Gen 12:4 to Gen 15
- The basis of this covenant was sacrifice. Gen 15
    - It was a covenant of grace.
    - It was a covenant of life.
    - Sacrifice was the ground of blessing; this was a type of the shed blood.
    - It guaranteed Israel's future and the re-establishment of Abraham's land - Canaan.
- Abraham believed God - Gen 15:6
    - He looked ahead to the cross.
    - This faith was accounted to him for righteousness.
    - He believed God for what He was going to do.
    - We believe God for what He has done. Heb 11:8-19
    - The condition for maintaining the blessing was simply to remain in the land of Canaan.

The Patriarchal Families
They were responsible for continuing the covenant, but they deteriorated.
- Abraham - Gen 12:11-13 (He lied.)
- Isaac - Gen 26:7 (He, too, lied.)
- Esau - Gen 25:32; 27:42 (He hated Jacob.)
- Jacob - Gen 27:19, 20; 42:1, 2; 45:28 (He lied and left Canaan.)

Joseph was sold into Egypt.
Results - judgment and the captivity in Egypt - Ex 1:1-14
Moses was born. Ex 2:1-10
- He delivered the children of Israel. Ex 2:23-25; 14:13-

16, 30-31
They arrive at Sinai.

The Age of the Law. Scriptural coverage of this age included Ex 19:3 to the Gospels

1. Length - from Mt Sinai to the Cross of Jesus - about 1558 years

2. Purposes of this age
    To show the foolishness of rejecting grace and choosing the Law; to see what is in the heart of man
    To reveal the purpose of the Law
    To prepare for Calvary
    To complete the writings of the Old Testament

3. Events of this age
    Israel was formally organized as a nation at Mt Sinai. (Ex 19)
        A theocracy which God led - Ex 13:17, 18; 15:3, 18
    Israel was a backslidden nation.
    Israel had become self-righteous and ignorant of God's Holiness; they thought God was dealing with them on their own merit.
    God had been dealing with them according to His covenant with Abraham.
    They promised to keep the Law. Ex 19:5-8
        "We will do," - not try or hope to do.
        God demanded perfect obedience.
        They did not know themselves and their own sin.
    The immediate result - Ex 19:9
        God veiled Himself; the Law separated them from a Holy God. Ex 19:12, 13
        Grace makes nigh to God. Gen 15:1; John 1:14,17, 18; 2 Cor 4:6; Ex 20:18 with Eph 2:13
    The Ten Commandments were given. Ex 20:1-17
    The purposes of the Law
        To Israel - Ex 20:20
            To prove them

To cause them to fear God
To keep them from sin
To prepare for Calvary
- Sacrifice (blood) - the ground of the Law Ex 20:24-26
- The Ark covered the law. Deut 10:1-5
- Christ is the end of the law. Gal 4:4,5

To us
- Brings us to Christ like a schoolmaster. Gal 3:19-24
- Gives us a knowledge of sin - Rom 3:20
- Shows grace is much better - Rom 5:20
- Shows our need for a Saviour

The Tabernacle was built in the wilderness. Ex 25:1-9; 35:1-10, 20-29; 36:1-7

The ceremonial law and priesthood were established. Book of Leviticus

The conquest and settlement in Canaan under Joshua took place.

The Book of Joshua

The period of the Judges who were leaders, counselors and deliverers took place.

For almost 400 years, God was King.

The Monarchy - I Samuel 8:4-7; 10:24

The reigns of Saul, David and Solomon brought the empire to its height.

But Israel backslid, and the kingdom was divided - man failed again.

The Ten Northern Tribes were taken captive into the Assyrian Captivity. 2 Kings 17:1-12, 20

Judah and Benjamin were taken captive by the Babylonians. 2 Kings 25:1-11

This was prophesied further. Luke 21:20-24

Most of the Old Testament was written during this period.
- Daniel prophesied and gave a picture of the Times of the Gentiles. about 600 B.C.
- Isaiah, Jeremiah, and Ezekiel - about 575 B.C., 780 B.C., and 626 B.C.

Hosea, Joel, Amos, Obadiah, Jonah - about 780 B.C.
Micah - about 750 B.C.
Nahum, Habakkuk, Zephaniah - about 630 B.C.
Haggai and Zechariah - about 520 B.C.
Malachi - about 488 B.C.

The Times of the Gentiles began 606 B.C.
- This was pictured by Daniel in Chapters 2 and 7.
- It began with Babylon, then Medo-Persia, then Greece, Rome and through the present age to the Second Coming of Christ.

The work of Jesus Christ - a work of regeneration
- Significance of the cross
  - The third phase in God's plan provided regeneration
  - The cross is the turning point of history.
  - The Old Testament saints were justified because they looked forward to the cross by faith.
  - The New Testament saints and Christians are justified because they look back to the cross by faith.

The prophetic meaning of the cross
- Old Testament teachings reveal that it is the blood which atones for sin, Lev 17:11 and animal sacrifices pointed to the coming Saviour and Messiah.
- They fulfilled Gen 3:15 that the seed of the woman would come from the nation of Israel, the tribe of Judah, and the family of David. 2 Sam 7:12-16

The revelation of the cross
- It revealed two classes of people—saved and unsaved.
- It exposed sin at its worst. Acts 2:23
- It revealed love at its best. John 3:16
- It revealed the wages of sin as separation from God (death). Rom 6:23; 5:12
- It revealed the agony of Jesus Who bore this separation.
- It vindicated the law of God.
  - God punishes sin and judges it.
    - Holiness cannot tolerate sin; justice demanded the punishment of sin.

It gave the supreme evidence of the love of God.
    In extent John 15:17
    In dying for the unholy and unlovely
The provisions of the cross - I Cor 1:30
    It provides redemption. I Peter 1:18, 19
    It provides justification, a new standing before God. Rom 3:24;5:1, 9
It provides righteousness which gives believers rights to God's presence. Rom 3:21, 22
It provides peace. Rom 5:1; Col 1:20; Eph 2:14, 15
It provides spiritual regeneration. John 3:3; 1:4; 10:10
It provides sanctification. Heb 13:12
It makes access to God possible. Heb 4:14-16; 10:19-22; Matt 27:51; Heb 7:25
It provides for glory to come. John17:24; Rev 7:13-15
It provides a way to balance the account for all sinners so that any and every last soul of Adam's race may lay claim.
    Up to this point the Old Testament saints balanced their sins with a sacrifice, thus revealing sorrow for sin, faith and obedience.
    On the cross Jesus made the last and full sacrifice for the sins of all ages and all men.
    The Creator's death balanced the account for all sinners so that any and every last soul could be saved.
    Finite man suffering for an infinite time equals infinite suffering;
        therefore

Infinite Man (Jesus) suffering for a finite time on the cross	Finite man (humanity) balances suffering for an infinite time, eternity

The accomplishments of the Cross
    It provided victory for man
        Sin brought guilt, but Jesus removed it. (2 Cor 5:21.
        Sin brought death, but Jesus died for us, giving us life.

John 10:10
Sin brought a "curse" upon man, but Jesus was made a curse for us. Gal 3:13
Sin brought the wrath of God against it, but Jesus bore that wrath. Rom 5:9

Jesus took over claim to the governorship of the Earth. Heb 1:1, 2
- The First Adam failed through disobedience; Jesus, as The Second Adam, succeeded by obedience.
- Jesus qualified as the Rightful Ruler and King of the earth.
- Satan was now a deposed foe of God and man.

Jesus led captivity captive. Eph 4:8
- He made possible the resurrection of the bodies of the saints.
- He freed the spirits of dead saints from Paradise, for He moved paradise to heaven when He rose from the dead.
- He preached to the spirits in prison. Eph 4:9; Rom10:7; I Peter 3:18-20;4:6
- He descended into Sheol.
- He preached to those who had died during the Anti-diluvian Age. I Peter 4:6
- (Refer to the Resurrection line on Chart No. One)
- He wrought judgment on sin. Rom 8:3; I Tim 5:24

The Resurrection of Christ (See line on Chart No. One)
- Its importance
  - God placed His approval upon the life and ministry of His Son.
  - It was proof to the world that Jesus was what He claimed to be.
  - He shall return to be King and World Ruler.
- Its significance
  - The Old Testament saints, upon death, went to the part of Sheol called Paradise.
  - Their bodies went into the grave, their spirits into Paradise. Luke 23:43

Psa 16:8-11 foretells His resurrection.

Peter and Paul quoted this prophecy to prove the resurrection. Acts 2:25-31; 13:32-37

The Hebrew word in Psa 16:10 is not "hell," and the Greek word in Acts 2:27 is "Hades."

Sheol and Hades are the same place.

It had two compartments: Paradise and torment. Luke 16:19-31

A great gulf was fixed between them. Luke 16:26

Paradise was a temporary "waiting place."
- Jesus said to the thief on the cross, "Today thou shalt be with me in Paradise"
- Three days later after His resurrection, Jesus had not been to heaven as He told Mary. John 20:17
- Jesus freed Old Testament saints from Paradise. Psa 68:18;Eph 4:7-10.
- You will remember that at the resurrection of Jesus, saints arose <u>with Him</u>, appeared in Jerusalem and were recognized. Matt 27:53
- Paradise since then has been in heaven.

The New Testament saints, upon death, go directly to heaven. 2 Cor 5:8

The body goes into the grave to await the Resurrection.

The first resurrection
- The spirits are with the Lord.

The unsaved dead
- The bodies go into the grave.
- The spirits go to the torment part of Sheol or Hades to await the second resurrection of the unsaved dead. Rev 20:4-15

The resurrection body of Jesus
- It was real flesh and bone. Lk 24:36-48; John 20:27
- Ours shall be like His. Phil 3:20; Psa 17:15; I John 3:2
- Flesh and blood cannot inherit the Kingdom, (I Cor 15:50) but flesh and bones can.
- It was a spiritual body(I Cor 15:52); an incorruptible body (Vs. 49); a recognizable body

        I Cor 13:12; I Thess 4:13-18;
        I John 3:2
Christ our High Priest in heaven (See Chart No.1, middle right)
    His ascension
        He ascended into heaven. Acts 1:9
        He promised to return. Acts 1:10,11
        He led captivity captive and gave gifts unto men.
    His present work for us in heaven: threefold
        He is our Advocate. I John 2:1, 2
        He is our High Priest. Heb 4:14
        He is our Intercessor. Heb 7:25
    Results of this work
        He gives us rest - through the new birth
            From committed sins - Matt 11:28
            From carnality - provides sanctification Heb 4:9
        We have ready access to His presence through prayer. Heb 4:15,16
        He prays for us. Heb 7:25; I Tim 2:5; I Pet 2:9 Rev 1:6
        He pleads for us when Satan accuses us. I John 2:1 Rom 8:33, 34
        He presents our worship, praise and prayer to God as our High Priest.
        He receives the confssion of our sins. I John 1:7, 9
        A picture of Him as High Priest Rev 1:12-20
        He sent the Holy Spirit. Acts 2
            Preparation - Acts 1:4, 5,12-14
            Sanctification - Acts 2
            Manifestation - Book of Acts
            This ushered in the dispensation of the Holy Spirit and introduced an Age of Grace.
The Jews during this period
    They were judged because they rejected Christ.
        In 70 A.D. Jerusalem was destroyed.
    The Jews were dispersed over the earth, continuing until now.
    God takes the scepter from the hands of the Jews and gives

it to the Gentiles.

A summary - we can summarize the function of the Scriptures, thusfar, as:
1. The Gospels - redemptive love manifested
2. Acts - redemptive news promoted
3. Epistles - redemptive truth proclaimed
4. Revelation - redemptive plans completed

<u>The Church Age</u>. Scriptural coverage of this age is Acts to Rev 4:1

1. Length - from Christ and Pentecost to the rapture of the Church (I Thess 4) - approximately 2000 years

2. The purposes of this age
    To test man under grace
    To build His Church - Eph 1:22
    To allow the Holy Spirit to work "within" man - John 14:17; Rom 8:9
    I Cor 3:16
    To evangelize (not convert) the world - Matt 28:18-20
    To reveal this is an age of the day of grace - John 3:16-19
        This is a mixed age. Matt 13
        This is the dispensation of the grace of God. Eph 3:1-6
        This was not made known in other ages. (Vs. 5, 6)
        God foreknew He would build His Church, and Paul revealed it. (Vs. 9)

3. The events of this age
    The history of this age is written in Rev 1-3.
    Christ, as Head of the Church, builds His Church. Eph 3:1-6; Matt 16:18; John 16:7; 7:37-39
    God takes out a people for His name. Acts 15:14-18
    It will be an age of testing - belief or rejection.
        To Jews - national acceptance or rejection of Jesus as Messiah and Saviour
        To Gentiles - as Saviour
    Acts 2 gives an account of the birthday of the Church.

Acts 10 and 11 give the record of the Church being extended to the Gentiles, also. Rom 1:16; I Cor 12:13, and Gal 3:28

4. The Church in relation to the Kingdom
   The Kingdom, unlike the Church, was no mystery.
   The Kingdom is earthly; the Church is heavenly.
   The Kingdom will be set up; the Church will be built.
   The Kingdom is coming.
      The Jews had a right to expect the Kingdom, but they looked for it at the wrong time.
   Jesus never denied a coming kingdom.

5. The relationship between Christ and the Church
   The Church is the body of Christ. Eph 1:17-23
   The Church is the Bride of Christ. 2 Cor 11:2 and Eph 5:23-30; Eph 2:4-6; Rev 19:7-10
   The Church is the temple of the Holy Spirit. I Cor 6:19, 20
   The Church is an eternal object lesson of grace. Eph 2:7

6. How to get into the Church
   By the new birth - John 3:3; 1:12
   By adoption into God's family
      Our prospect Rev 5:10
      Our duty - to witness for Him, to win others and to wait for His coming 2 Timothy 2:2

7. This age will end in apostasy and judgment. 2 Thess 2
   The mixed character of this age is seen by the study of the parables of Jesus in Matt 13.
   Result - apostasy, a falling away - Lk 17:26-32; 21:25.26; 18:18;
   2 Pet 2:1; 3:4; 2 Tim 3:1-7
   The true Church will be delivered out of this age to escape judgment.
      <u>I Thess 4:17, 18</u>; John 14:1-3; 5:28, 29; Matt 24:27, 36, 40, 41, 43; 25:1-13; 25:19-30; I Cor 15:51, 52
   After the Church is gone, judgment will strike. Lk 21:25-36;

Divine Imperatives

2 Thess 2:7-12

8. The Jews
   They are dispersed into all the world in unbelief because they crucified Jesus and were blind. Rom 11:25
   Jerusalem was destroyed and trodden down by the Gentiles in 70 A.D.

9. The times of the Gentiles will cease. Rom 11:25
10. The entire New Testament was written.

End Time Prophecies and Future Ages

Chart 4

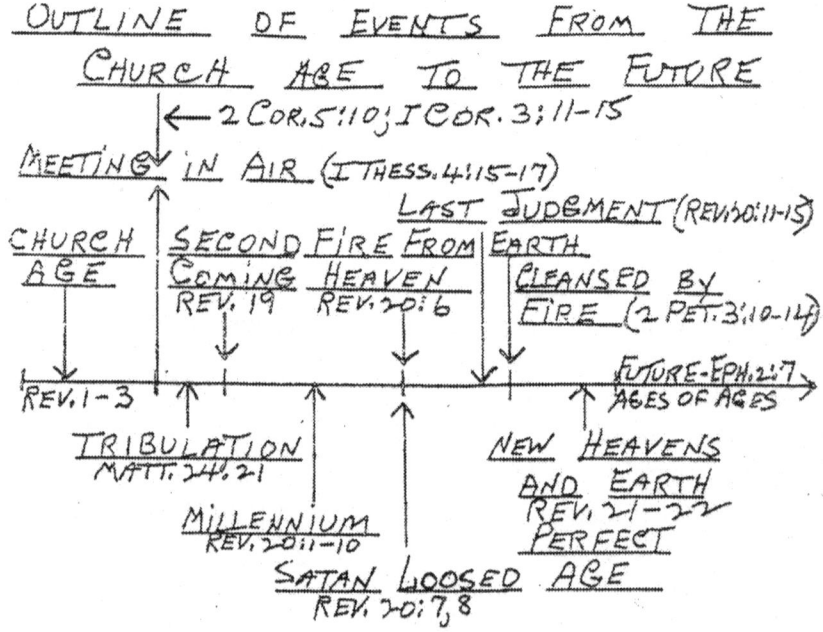

End Time Events

(Consult the Rapture Line, Chart No. 4 between Church and Tribulation)

<u>The Rapture of the Church</u>. At the end of the Church Age, Christ will come <u>for</u> His Church. A short time later He will come <u>with</u> His Church.

Judgment ends the Church Age, and a period of Tribulation will come, but the Church will escape this Tribulation. I Thess 1:10; 2 Thess 2:7, 8 The Church will be translated to heaven. I Thess 4:17

Why a translation?

1. That sin may come to a head - the cup of iniquity will be full
2. That the Church may escape the purifying judgments of a God-defying, God-rejecting world

> The "dead in Christ" will rise first.
> The living Christians will be translated.
> The resurrected and translated Christians will rise together to meet the Lord <u>in the air</u>.

A period of tribulation, conducted by the Antichrist, will follow. There will be tribulation saints in the immediate three and one-half years that follow. They, too, will be resurrected and translated into heaven. At that time the Times of the Gentiles will cease.

<u>The Judgment Seat of Christ.</u> Scriptures revealing this event include 2 Cor 5:10; Rom 14:10; I Cor 3:11-15. What will take place?

> Only Christians will be there.
> Sinners will be judged later. Rev 20:11-15
> These two judgments are 1000 years apart.
> The works of Christians will be tried. 2 Cor 5:10; I Cor 3:11-15
> > Two kinds of works will be judged: (1) jewels and (2) chaff.
> > Chaff works will be burnt up.
> > Gold stands for Deity.
> > > We build gold when we exalt Jesus as Son of God.
> > Silver stands for redemption.
> > > We build silver when we tell the story of redemption.
> > Precious stones stand for souls won. Mal 3:17

We build stones with every soul we win.
Rewards will be given on the basis of merit. I Cor 3:11-15
    The Crown of Life - Jas 1:12
    The Incorruptible Crown - I Cor 9:25
    The Crown of Glory - I Pet 5:4
    The Martyr's Crown - Rev 2:10
    The Crown of Rejoicing - I Thess 2:19, 20
God's ways with Christians will be vindicated. I Cor 13:12; Rom 8:18
All mysteries will be understood.
All problems will be solved.
Christians will be assigned places of service in the Millennial Age to follow.
They will be rulers.

<u>The Marriage Supper of the Lamb.</u> Rev 19:7-9 This will probably follow the Judgment Seat while the Tribulation is in progress on earth. The Bride has made herself ready - Rev 19:7. There will be guests at the wedding, Old Testament saints. Jesus is crowned and Satan dethroned. The Tribulation saints will also be present at the wedding. Rev 19:9

<u>The Tribulation on Earth.</u> This is a time of judgment of heaven on earth. The Jews will be judged for rejecting Christ; this is called the Time of Jacob's Trouble which will last for seven years. Jer 30:4-7; Dan 12:1; Matt 24:21; Dan 7:21, 25; 11:36; Joel 2:2, 31; Zech 1:17, 18 It will also be a time of tribulation for the Gentiles at the end of the period for the way they have treated the Jews. Matt 31-46

    The Antichrist, Beast and False Prophet will reign during this time of tribulation, but they will be ultimately destroyed. 2 Thess 2:8

    The Jews will be revived nationally (Ezek 39:1-14) and spiritually through the work of 144,000 evangelists and two witnesses. Rev 7 and 11; Ezek 36:24-27; 37:15-28; Rom 11:25-27; Zech 12:10-14; 13:1, 2, 6.

    Then the Tribulation will end with the Second Coming of Christ and the Battle of Armageddon.

<u>The Second Coming</u> (Revelation) <u>of Christ with His Church</u>. Rev 19:11-16;

> Mal 4; Dan7..
> It was prophesied. Jude 14; John 4:1, 2
> It will occur at the end of the Tribulation. Matt 24:29, 30
> Jesus wins the Battle of Armageddon. Zech 14:4; Isa 63:1-6; Rev 19; 2 Thess 2:8; Rev 20:1-3
> He judges the Gentile nations. Matt 25:31-46
> Here He fulfills Daniel's Smiting Stone. Dan7
> The Sheep and Goat Judgment is based on the way the nations have treated the Jews.
> The Jews are converted and restored. Isa 53:1-9; Zech 12:10; Hosea 5:15; 6:1-3; Matt 23:37-39; Acts 3:19-21
> The Antichrist, Beast and False Prophet are judged and cast into the Lake of Fire. Rev 19:20
> Satan will be bound for 1000 years. Rev 20:1-8

<u>The Age of the Millennium.</u> To study this age, refer to Charts 1 and 4. Scriptures which cover this period are Rev 20:1-8
   1. Length - 1000 years from the Second Coming
   2. Purposes of this age
      To give Jesus the King the opportunity to rule as Earth Governor
      To regenerate the physical earth
      To keep His promises to Abraham and David
      To convert the world
   3. The events of the Millennium
      Glory for Christ
      He will be world Governor. Isa 9:6, 7
      He will be King of Kings. Psa 2:6; Heb 1:8, 9; Psa 45:6, 7; 72:8
      A restored Jerusalem will be capital of the world.
      Christ will rule in righteousness and love. Isa 11:1, 4; Rev 2:27; 19:15; Psa 2:9
   Glory for the Church - Col 3:4; I Thess 4:17; Rom 8:16-18; Rev 1:6

Resurrected bodies - I John 3:2; Phil 3:21
We shall reign with Him. 2 Tim 2:12
The 12 Apostles will rule. Matt 19:28; Isa 1:26
The responsibilities will be service. Lk 19:11-26
Glory for Israel
    Regathered in Palestine to keep God's promises to Abraham
        Ezek 37:1-4; 37:21; Isa 11; 14:11; Jer 16:14, 15; 30:11; 32:41
    Reconciled to Christ as Messiah - Zech 12; 13; 14:4
        Praised in all lands - Zech 3:14-20
        Chosen as religious leaders of the world - Zech 8:2-8; 8:23;
        Isa 2:1-3; Ezek 48; 40:1; 44:15-31
        Jerusalem established as the world capital - Isa 1:26; Zech 8:4, 5
        David elected King of Israel - Ezek 37:15-28; Jer 30:9
Glory for certain Gentile nations - Matt 25:31-34, 39
    Basis:"brethren" and "Gospel" - Matt 24:14; 25:34ff
    There will be world peace. Isa 2:4; Micah 4:3
Glory for the physical creation
        The earth will be regenerated. Isa 55:13; 35:1, 2, 6, 7 Ezek 36:25; Rom 8:13-22; Amos 9:13; Matt 10:27, 28
        Wild beasts will be made tame. Isa 11:1-14; Rom 8:21; Hosea 2:18; Isa 65:25; 35:7
Satan will be bound for 1000 years. Rev 20:1-3
    If there is a rebellion, Jesus will deal with it on the spot.
    Carnality in mankind will still be present but held in subjection.

4. Events which follow the Millennium
    After 1000 years Satan will be loosed to make one final test
    Why?
        To prove the incorrigibility of Satan
        To show the absolute justice of God in casting the

wicked into the Lake of Fire forever
To try those who were born during the Millennium
To show that the natural man will rebel and needs the new birth
What happens: - Rev 20:9, 10
   Fire destroys them. Vs. 9
   Satan will be cast into the Lake of Fire. Vs.10

The Final Judgment of the Great White Throne Rev 20:1-15

Jesus is the Great Judge. Vs.11; John 5:22; Acts 10:42; 17:31
Who shall be judged?
   Not Christians - John 5:24, R.V.
   But the unsaved dead - Vs. 12
   Also fallen angels and demons - Jude 6
How will they be judged?
   No partiality - Vs. 12; Rom 14:11; Phil 2:9-11
   Degrees of punishment determined
      Some with many stripes; some with few stripes
         Matt 11:22, 24; Lk 12: 41-48, according to works
      By God's perfect records - Vs. 12
      Book of Remembrance - Mal 3:16; Psa 39:4; 56:8; Eccles 12:14
      Book of Conscience - Rom 2:14-16
      Book of the Law - Rom 2:11, 12; Gal 3:10
      Book of God's Eternal Counsel - Psa 139:16
      Book of Life - Vs. 12b and Vs. 15

The New Heavens and the New Earth. -Rev 21:1-5

This is the phase of sanctification.
The earth will be sanctified with a baptism of fire similar to that which sanctifies the heart of the regenerated believer. 2 Pet 3:7-10 How? - Rev 21:1
   Word here in the Greek means paerchomai, to pass from one condition to another.
   The restored earth will be cleansed by fire.

All regions where fallen angels and man have worked against God will be cleansed by fire.

The Events of the Future

(See extreme right on Chart No.One)

The Great Abdication. I Cor 15:24-28

The Son of God will give back the Kingdom to God the Father, but before that He will have put down all rule, authority, or power and all enemies under His feet.

The sin question is settled and earth is immune from rebellion and sin.

There will be complete restoration, both for the earth and man. All that was lost in Adam will be completely and absolutely regained.

The Ages to Come. Eph 2:7

The Perfect Age - Rev 21-22

    This includes the new heaven and new earth.

    It includes the new Jerusalem and the restored Paradise, purified by fire. 2 Peter 3:7; Isa 65:17

    It will be a sinless kingdom without rebels or apostates which Christ will deliver to the Father. Zech 14:20; Dan 7:13, 14, 27; I Cor 15:24, 28

    Christ will be all in all. Phil 2:9-11; Eph 1:20-23

    Without sin, it will be of full age. Eph 1:10

Length

    Israel will have a large place for 1000 generations or about 33,000 years. Isa 66:22; Deut 7:9

Characteristics of these ages

    No sin, disease, storms, or death will plague inhabitants.

    No more sea will exist.

    The earth will blossom, and the meek shall inherit it.

There will be a prepared city. John 14:1-4; Rev 21-22:6
    It will be the New Jerusalem that comes down from heaven.
God will live with men. Rev 21:3, 4
Men will probably populate the universe. Jas 1:18; Isa 9:17

<u>The Ages to Come</u> (unlimited future eternity)
    The Kingdom of God which is absolutely holy
    The ages to come - Eph 2:4-7
        These are the Omega Ages.
        Time ceases, and the ages of the ages begin. Eph 3:21
        The servants of God shall reign for the ages of the ages. Rev 20:10
        The future is unknown, but Paul says that wonderful things lie ahead. I Cor 2:9

www.ingramcontent.com/pod-product-compliance
Lightning Source LLC
LaVergne TN
LVHW041532070526
838199LV00046B/1625

www.ingramcontent.com/pod-product-compliance
Lightning Source LLC
LaVergne TN
LVHW041532070526
838199LV00046B/1625